Once Upon a Time in Africa

Stories of Wisdom and Joy

D1531197

Once Upon a Time in Africa

Stories of Wisdom and Joy

Compiled by Joseph G. Healey

ORBIS BOOKS
Maryknoll, New York 10545

Second Printing, January 2005

Founded in 1970, Orbis Books endeavors to publish works that enlighten the mind, nourish the spirit, and challenge the conscience. The publishing arm of the Maryknoll Fathers and Brothers, Orbis seeks to explore the global dimensions of the Christian faith and mission, to invite dialogue with diverse cultures and religious traditions, and to serve the cause of reconciliation and peace. The books published reflect the views of their authors and do not represent the official position of the Maryknoll Society. To learn more about Maryknoll and Orbis Books, please visit our website at www.maryknoll.org.

Published by Orbis Books, Maryknoll, New York 10545-0308.
Manufactured in the United States of America.

Library of Congress Cataloging-in-Publication Data

Once upon a time in Africa : stories of wisdom and joy / compiled by Joseph G. Healey.
　　p. cm.
　ISBN 1-57075-527-2 (pbk.)
　1. Christian life—Catholic authors. 2. Folklore—Africa,
Sub-Saharan. I. Healey, Joseph G.
　BX2350.3 .O53 2004
　276—dc22
　　　　　　　　　　2003019931

In Gratitude to the African People

our ancestors of the distant past
our recent living dead
our living
our yet unborn

Contents

Morocco

Tunisia

Algeria

Libya

Egypt

Western Sahara

Cape Verde

Mauritania

Mali

Niger

Chad

Sudan

Eritrea

Senegal

Djibouti

Gambia

Burkina Faso

Nigeria

Ethiopia

Somalia

Guinea-Bissau

Guinea

Benin

Sierra Leone

Côte d'Ivoire

Ghana

Togo

Liberia

Cameroon

Central African Republic

Equatorial Guinea

Congo

Uganda

Kenya

Sao Tome and Principe

Gabon

Democratic Republic of Congo

Rwanda

Burundi

Tanzania

Seychelles

Angola

Malawi

Comoros

Mayotte

Saint Helena

Zambia

Mozambique

Madagascar

Mauritius

Zimbabwe

Réunion

Namibia

Botswana

Swaziland

Lesotho

South Africa

Map by Global Mapping International 10/03 - www.gmi.org

Introduction

Once upon a time...

And so a story begins, and the storyteller weaves his or her magical art. In Africa, traditionally, the elders would gather the young people and children around the fire at night and narrate the stories, history, and events that made them a proud and memorable people. These stories tell us who we are and help us to maintain and deepen our identity. Stories help define and sustain individuals, families, and, indeed, nations.

Once upon a time—and it was the beginning of all eternity—God our Creator and Source began the work of creation. God's Spirit went to every part of creation—the galaxies, the stars, the planets—and the seeds of God were planted everywhere. The Unsurpassed Great Spirit scattered seeds of love, peace, truth, and hope far and wide among a great diversity of peoples, cultures, and religious traditions.

Throughout Africa there is widespread belief in one Supreme God. In many places in Africa the one High God speaks through the world religion of Islam, in others through African religion, and in still others through the various forms of Christianity, including the African-initiated churches. Before the first European missionaries arrived in Africa, the Supreme Being had already visited the people whom the High God knows and loves. African religious heritage and culture have always been privileged places of God's revelation. The proverbs and myths of the African people reveal that the Holy Spirit sowed the seeds of the Good News in African cultures long before the African people ever heard Jesus' words and teachings.

These stories from Africa tell of compassion, conversion, forgiveness, grace, joy, mercy, peace, reconciliation, repentance, and unity. They probe deeply into the human heart, into the mystery of being, and into human relationships with God and with others. They plunge into the depths and reach to the skies in the eternal quest for meaning.

"Story," as I'm using it here, includes many different forms of African oral and written literature, including folktales, historical fiction, legends, myths, parables, poems, prayers, proverbs, sayings, and songs. I have also drawn true stories from African history and mission experience in Africa, my own and that of others. Real-life stories—those that tell of real people and events —have their own power to inspire, uplift, and challenge.

From these stories, the origins of which range from South Africa and Kenya in East Africa to Burkina Faso and Nigeria in West Africa, certain African values clearly emerge. While people in every culture are able to overcome adversity, the special gift or charism of Africans is to be joyful and to celebrate amidst such problems as AIDS, corruption, disease, famine, persecution, poverty, violence, and war. Julius Nyerere, the first president of Tanzania, once said, "In Africa we have problems, but we remain cheerful."

I hope these African stories will shed some light on your own spiritual journey. For, after all, once upon a time and for all time, the journey is one.

I would like to thank and acknowledge the authors and collectors mentioned at the end of each story. Special thanks go to Father Donald Sybertz, M.M. and Mr. John Mbonde.

Joseph G. Healey, M.M.
Dar es Salaam, Tanzania
October 1, 2003

In the Beginning

"All that God has created is good."
Akan proverb from Ghana

The nature of God is a mystery. Traditional African religion acknowledges God as the One Creator and Sustainer of all things. It speaks of God's eternal nature, which distinguishes God from what God has created. It also speaks about God's relation to creation, especially to humankind. Many of the best known scientific theories of the origins of humankind assert that indeed we came from Africa, from around the Olduvai Gorge in the Serengeti in northwestern Tanzania or from South Africa or from Chad.

Because nearly all African ethnic groups have creation myths or myths of origin, more than two thousand exist. They tell of the creation of the universe, the earth, animals, and especially human beings. They also describe the separation of God and human beings. Unlike the story of creation and the fall in the Bible, where humans were driven from Paradise by God, most African versions tell of how God withdrew into heaven because human beings did something wrong. Some of these stories also describe the origin of death.

Here are some African stories of how the world came to be.

The Myth of Man and the Elephant

Once upon a time in Africa, God created man and an elephant. These he put in a beautiful garden and he walked with them every day. Pure water for drinking flowed in a river until the elephant started muddying the waters. He would listen to neither God nor man who told him to stop. In the end, man killed the elephant. God, though, was upset at this act and drove man out of the garden.

Hence it is that the Borana people in Ethiopia and Kenya now live in a ceaseless search for water in drought-stricken lands.

Myth, Borana-Oromo ethnic group, Ethiopia/Kenya,
collected by Father Alexander Chima

A Dinka Myth of the Beginning

God created in the beginning a man and a woman, and the earth was so near to the sky that people on earth could easily reach God in the sky by a rope that stretched between them. Sickness and death were unknown, and a single grain of millet was sufficient for a day's food. God forbade them to pound more than this single grain. The woman, however, wanted more food and she began to pound more grain with the long-handled pestle the Dinka use. In doing so, she struck God, who withdrew to the heights and sent a finch to sever the rope that had once allowed man easy access to him. Therefore man has since had to work hard to get his food, and death and sickness, unknown when God and man were near together, are his lot.

An ancient Dinka myth, Sudan,
recounted by Godfred Lienhardt in Laurenti Magesa's
African Religion: The Moral Traditions of Abundant Life
(Maryknoll, N.Y.: Orbis Books, 1997)

Leeyio's Mistake

There was once a man known as Leeyio. He was the first man that Naiteru-kiop [literally "The Beginner of the Earth"] brought to earth. Naiteru-kiop called Leeyio and said to him, "When a person dies and you dispose of the corpse, you must remember to say, 'Person die and come back again, moon die and remain away.'"

Many months elapsed before anyone died. When, in the end, a neighbor's child died, Leeyio was summoned to dispose of the body. When he took the corpse outside, he made a mistake and said, "Moon die and come back again, person die and stay away." So, after that, no person survived death.

A few more months elapsed, and then Leeyio's own child went "missing." So the father took the corpse outside and said, "Moon die and remain away, person die and come back again."

On hearing this, Naiteru-kiop said to Leeyio, "You are too late, for, through your own mistake, death was born the day your neighbor's child died."

That is how death came about, and that is why up to this day when a person dies he or she does not return, but when the moon dies, it always comes back again.

Myth, Maasai ethnic group, Kenya/Tanzania

Kaonde Myth of Creation

God created two people, Mulonga and Mwinambuzhi, who were to become the first man and woman. When God created them, they had not yet been differentiated into male and female. In fact, they were lacking in the things that would enable them to relieve themselves. This made them very uncomfortable. Mulonga went to God to seek help. When God heard their problems, he realized that he had left out some important things. So he gave Mulonga two small packets and said, "One is yours and one is for Mwinambuzhi. Take them home, and before you go to bed, put one packet in your crotch and tell your companion to place the other packet in her crotch."

Mulonga took the packets and began his journey home immediately. However, the journey was a long one and he became very weary. He lay down and went to sleep, but, before he slept, he put his packet in his crotch.

When he got up, in the morning, he was surprised. He had been changed into a male and the other things that he had lacked had also been provided. He picked up the packet that he had been ordered to give to Mwinambuzhi, but he noticed that it had a bad odor and he threw it away, saying, "It's rotten—and besides, it's heavy."

He continued on his journey and, when he arrived home, Mwinambuzhi noticed that he had been changed. So she asked him, "What happened to you?"

Mulonga told her what God had instructed him to do, but did not tell her about the packet that God had sent to her.

Mwinambuzhi decided to go to God and get some medicine too. When she found God, she told him of her problem. God said in surprise, "Didn't Mulonga give you the packet I sent along for you?"

Mwinambuzhi replied, "No, he didn't. He told me only about his packet."

So God gave Mwinambuzhi another packet along with instructions. She followed the instructions and when she awoke in the morning she found her all missing parts.

Then something new happened to them. They desired each other and they had intercourse. However, afterwards they felt strange and afraid of this new thing of knowing one another. They decided to go to God and tell him about it because they had their doubts. God heard what they said and told them not to fear knowing one another, because this was the way in which they would conceive and bear children. After that, Mulonga and Mwinambuzhi bore many children. They cared for them and their family grew. Their children were the parents of many clans.

One day God said to Mulonga, "Why did you not carry out the orders I gave you regarding the packet for your companion? Why did you throw hers away?" Then God said, "You did a bad thing when you did that. Therefore, as punishment from now on, when a man marries a woman, he will have to pay a dowry."

Myth, Kaonde ethnic group, Zambia,
collected by Father John Ganly, M.M.

The Honey Bird and the Three Gourds

Time passed. One day God called Mayimba, the Honey Bird, who was a friend of our ancestors. God gave Mayimba three gourds that were plugged up. He said, "Go to the man and woman I created and give them these three gourds. But you are not to open them on the way. When you get to their village, you are to tell them, 'Open this first gourd with the seeds of all things and plant them for food, but do not open these other gourds until I come. When I come I will tell you what to do with the other two.'"

Mayimba began the long journey. He grew overwhelmed with curiosity about the contents of the gourds, so he stopped and opened the first gourd with the seeds. When he verified that such was the content, he put them back in the gourd and plugged it up again.

Then he opened the second gourd. It contained medicine for curing death, illness, and tiredness and for calming wild and dangerous animals. But no one had ever experienced these things, so Mayimba did not know what they were. He put the medicine back into the gourd and replugged it.

When he got to the third gourd, he found that it was filled with death, disease, and dangerous animals. When he opened it, they all escaped and dispersed throughout the world. Mayimba tried in vain to recapture them and return them to the gourd.

Eventually, God came as he had promised, and when God saw what Mayimba had done, he became exceedingly angry. Together they tried to recapture the bad things Mayimba had let loose, but they were unable to do so.

God was furious with Mayimba, and said to him, "You did very, very badly. It is your fault." When Mayimba heard this, he was very frightened and escaped into the wilderness. From that time on, he ceased to live in the village of his friends.

Then God called the first man, Mulonga, and his wife Mwinambuzhi, and said, "Your friend Mayimba has done a great evil in failing to follow my instructions about waiting to open the gourds until I came. He has caused you great trouble. I am unable to repair what he has done. However, I will teach you how to sew clothes and build houses wherein you can stay and protect yourselves."

He taught them to kill wild animals and to use their skins. He taught them to smelt copper. He taught them to make fire with two dry sticks. He taught them to make axes and spears and pots for cooking and collecting water. He taught them all things.

Myth, Kaonde ethnic group, Zambia,
collected by Father John Ganly, M.M.

The Myth of the Inquisitive Hunter

A very long time ago in Africa, God, named Ghitema, lived very near the world of human beings. God was with the people and totally involved in their affairs, helping them in their work and assisting them in their daily tasks. The people did not feel the hardships of life. In order to maintain this harmony, human beings were absolutely forbidden to shoot their arrows into the sky. Ghitema told them it would disrupt the entire tranquility of life.

One member of the hunter clan was very inquisitive about the sky. He wanted to know whether it was so hard that an arrow could not penetrate it or whether it was as soft as butter. So—against the command of God—this hunter shot an arrow into the sky. The sky immediately started to bleed and moved far up, away from the earth's surface. God also went far away.

From that day on, people started to feel the hardships of life. There was no link between human beings on earth and their God on high. This is why people introduced the practice of spirits as intermediaries to present their needs to God, with each spirit having its own special function. Various sacrifices were offered to God through the spirits in order to attain God's favor. So it is today.

Myth, Ngoreme ethnic group, Tanzania,
collected by Father Matei Mung'aho,
Towards An African Narrative Theology
(Orbis Books, 1996)

The Chameleon and the Rabbit

A long time ago, the animal world was divided into kingdoms. At that time, the cheetah was the king of the small animals such as rabbits, tortoises, lizards, rats, worms, snails, and chameleons. The king wanted to make his subjects more active. So, he announced that there was to be a big marathon. Whoever came first in this race would marry his daughter.

The animals practiced for a long time in preparation for the race. All of them were pleased with their progress except for the snails, the worms, and the chameleons, who didn't seem to be improving much.

As the months passed, each animal planned various strategies for the big day. The chameleon discovered while he was practicing that he had a special talent for grasping, gripping, and holding. He was also very smart.

The day for the race came. The king lowered the flag at the starting line and the race was on! The rabbit took off at a fast pace and was soon ahead of all the other animals. He realized he was winning by a large margin and so, just for the fun of it, he stopped to take a little nap by the side of the road.

When the rabbit awoke, he ran straight for the chair that had been specially prepared for the winner. As soon as he reached the chair, he sat on it at once. He was elated at the thought of marrying the king's daughter.

Then he heard a soft voice and felt something alive under him on the seat of the chair. He turned and looked. There— attached to his bottom and half squeezed out of existence—was the chameleon!

"Friend," the chameleon said, "do not sit on me. I arrived on this seat before you."

Folktale, Kikuyu ethnic group, Kenya,
collected by Sister Ephigenia Gachiri, I.B.V.M.,
Nairobi, Kenya

Life

"Life is the best gift; the rest is extra."
Swahili proverb from Eastern and Central Africa

Central to the African worldview is the value of life itself. This "vital force" is described as abundant life, the fullness of life. Many stories of everyday life in Africa portray the humor, vibrancy, energy, and creativity of the people and their culture. As a rule, Africans take life as it is. They play the cards they are dealt and don't feel sorry for themselves. They make the best of their lives despite daily struggles, widespread sickness, and often harsh environmental conditions. They feel God's presence in their lives and are optimistic.

At the same, death is an important part of the African worldview. Many proverbs, myths, folktales, stories, and songs tell about death, focusing often on the transitory nature of life on earth. All people who are alive are also on the verge of dying. Death is seen as part of living. It is nondiscriminatory and universal; eventually it claims everybody.

This emphasis on the fullness of life is significant for African Christians. In some parts of Africa, Jesus is named the "One from Whom All Life Flows" or "Proto-Ancestor." This latter title for Jesus also reflects the African belief in the continuity of life, which includes the not-yet-born, the living, and the "living dead." The "vital force" of life is greatly valued, but death, in the end, does not totally separate the dead from the living.

Here, then, is a taste of life in Africa.

I Am the Dancing Man

In a small village in southern Africa, near a river, there once lived an orphan boy named Joseph. When he was still very small, Joseph knew that life in the village was dreary and hard. No one laughed. No one danced. But Joseph could see that everywhere around him the world danced. Fire danced near the village huts. Trees swayed in the wind. Clouds danced in the sky.

One evening as he was standing by the river, Joseph met an old man. He was wearing silver sandals and was "dancing the waves." The old man swept off his hat and bowed. "I am the Dancing Man," he said, "and I have a gift for you."

The gift was his pair of silver sandals, and before long Joseph began to dance, taking the old man's place. He danced from village to village and people responded. An old woman gave him a flower, and Joseph danced with the flower. He met a young child who was ill and in pain and, as he danced, the young girl smiled. He met a farmer who was sowing seeds. Joseph danced, and the farmer danced with him as he sowed. Wherever Joseph danced, there was life—until the day came when he was old.

Then one day Joseph looked up and saw standing by the river a young boy waiting, as long ago he had waited. The boy drew near. Joseph knew the words to say. He swept off his hat and bowed. "I am the Dancing Man," he said, "and I have a gift for you."

Parable, Brother Carmine, S.M., Southern Africa
(Challenge *Magazine*)

Journey of Two Old Men Called Life and Death

Two old men journeyed together. The name of one was Life and the name of the other was Death.

When they came to a place where a spring flowed, the man who owned the spring greeted them. They asked permission to drink. He said, "Yes, drink. But the elder should drink first, because that is the custom."

Life said, "I, indeed, am the elder."

Death said, "No, I am the elder."

Life answered, "But how can that be? Life came first. Without living things to die, Death does not exist."

Death responded, "On the contrary, before Life was born, everything was Death. Living things come out of Death, continue awhile, and then return to Death."

Life rejoined, "Surely that is not the way it is. Before Life there was no Death, merely that which was not seen. The Creator made this world out of unseen substances. When the first person died, that was the beginning of Death. Therefore you, Death, are the younger."

Death argued, "Death is merely what we do not know. In the beginning, when the Creator created, he molded everything out of what we do not know. Therefore, Death is like a father to Life."

They spent a long time disputing in this way. At last, they asked the owner of the spring to judge the dispute.

He said, "How can one speak of Death without Life,

from which it proceeds? And how can one speak of Life without Death, to which all living things go? Both of you have spoken eloquently. Your words are true. Neither one of you can exist without the other. Neither of you is senior, neither is junior. Life and Death are merely two faces of the Creator. Therefore, you are of equal age. Here is a gourd of water. Drink from it together."

They received the gourd of water, drank from it, and then continued on their journey.

Myth, Hausa ethnic group, Nigeria,
collected by Father John Halbert, M.M.

We Have a Debt to Pay

Mr. Matolo is a paraplegic Xhosa man, in his mid-fifties, who is permanently disabled as the result of a car accident. Life as a paraplegic in rural South Africa presents many challenges, not only because of poverty and the lack of resources, but also because of cultural beliefs, such as curses, and the role of men in society.

Mr. Matolo was able to return to work in the orthopedic hospital as a craft teacher. The government provided him free accommodation consisting of a small room, but it was far from the hospital and difficult to access by car. He relied on the good will of the hospital driver who drove him back and forth to work. More times than not, though, he waited for hours and no vehicle came.

So, Mr. Matolo decided to work extra jobs such as repairing shoes and selling crafts to earn enough to build a house near the hospital. His dream was finally achieved and he could use his wheelchair to get to work every day.

Mr. Matolo has always been present to his neighbors. When the women in his neighborhood needed day care for their children because they had found jobs in town, he brought the families together to build a small hut where women who were not working could take turns watching the children. Mr. Matolo still takes on extra jobs to earn money for this project.

When it was time for us to leave South Africa, my suitcase needed repair. I thought that I could use the occasion to give some extra money to the day care project, so I took my suitcase to Mr. Matolo. When it was time to pay, he refused to accept my money. He just said that I could pay him when I returned.

At that time we weren't sure where our future would lead us, but Mr. Matolo must have known. We are now on our way back. We have a debt to pay.

True story, Monica Vega and Heidi Schmidt, Umtata, South Africa

The Peacock and the Vulture

The vulture was once king of all the birds, but he was an oppressive king. The birds could not build their nests without permission from him, and in order to get this permission they had to work hard for the vulture and his family. This went on for a long time and everyone got used to the situation.

After a long time had passed, the family of the eagles revolted. This didn't lead to any change, though, because the vulture sent them into exile, and they were permitted to fly no lower than an iroko tree. Then the family of the hens revolted and they were also banned from flying. Soon all the birds gave up their attempts to resist the oppressive rule of the vulture.

Unbeknownst to the rest of the birds, however, the family of the peacock had grown close to the vulture. He was glad to be associated with a family of such beautiful birds. One day, contrary to the will of the dove, the god of the birds, the vulture married the peacock. Because the peacock was a very good cook, the family of the vulture came to love her very much.

One day, the peacock prepared a delicious meal for the vulture and his greedy family. They all ate the meal and they all died because the food had been poisoned. Thus, the beautiful lady peacock liberated the whole kingdom of the birds.

Folktale, Ika ethnic group, Nigeria

You'd Better Be Running

Every morning in Africa, when a gazelle wakes up it knows it must run faster than the fastest lion or it will be killed.

Every morning in Africa, when a lion wakes up it knows it must outrun the slowest gazelle or it will starve to death.

It doesn't matter whether you're a lion or a gazelle. When the sun comes up, you'd better be running.

Popular story, Africa,
collected by Father Ted Hayden, S.M.A.

Athanasius Evangelized Me with a Cup of Tea

One day Bishop Christopher Mwoleka came to our house in Nyabihanga village in Rulenge, Tanzania, on an unexpected visit. My good friend Athanasius and I hurriedly prepared tea for the villagers who came to greet the bishop. We started with two full thermoses, but then several other visitors came and soon we had finished all the tea. I wondered what I would do if another person came.

Just then, one of our neighbors arrived to say hello. As I started to apologize for not having any more tea, Athanasius spontaneously picked up his own cup of tea and politely handed it to the visitor. It was a simple gesture of sharing, but for me a profound act of love and beauty. By his example, Athanasius had evangelized me.

True story, Father Joseph Healey, M.M., Nyabihanga, Tanzania,
A Fifth Gospel: The Experience of Black Christian Values
(Orbis Books, 1981)

The Medicine Pouch

The southern African village of Ha Sethoto was ruled by a strong but foolish headman who decided to break away from the rule of King Poelano, even though the king treated everyone fairly and well. The king could easily have destroyed the village, but instead he sent his oldest adviser to sit down with the elders under the baobab tree and reason with them.

The king's representative said that he had been sent to invite the village to return to the kingdom and that the king was very concerned about them. Had the king offended them in some way? Had he oppressed them? What was wrong? What could he do to make it right?

The elders were too embarrassed to admit that they had no real grievances against the good king. So, they tried to cover up their embarrassment with anger. They lashed out with defiant words, but the messenger stayed calm, which infuriated them even more. Finally, they became so enraged that they viciously beat the king's messenger and killed him. Like butchers, they drained his blood into a clay pot and sent it to King Poelano as their reply to his invitation.

A terrible wailing went up as the news spread throughout King Poelano's village. Everyone expected the king to send his warriors immediately to deal with this horrible insult. Their spears and arrows could easily wipe out the village of Ha Sethoto. They could burn all its houses and maize fields as an example to other villages. Then people would know what happens to people who flaunt their disrespect for the king.

However, the king did something completely different, something unforgettable, something that showed his real nature. There was a huge flat rock where he always stood when he called together leaders from all across his kingdom. He went out to the rock, poured the blood of his messenger onto it, and waited for the blood to dry under the hot African sun. Then he ground the dried blood to powder and put it into a medicine pouch made of lambskin.

He sent the pouch to the rebellious village with this message: "The blood of the messenger you killed is in this medicine pouch. It may bring you life or death. Though you killed him, I still invite you to come back into my kingdom on one condition. You must take some of the dried blood of my messenger, mix it with water, and rub it on your hands. Then come, stand before me at the great flat rock, and hold up your hands. In this way you will admit that you killed my messenger but that you now want to be received back into my kingdom. I declare that if you trust me and wear the blood of the messenger you killed, his blood will be the means of reconciliation between us and I will welcome you back into my kingdom. There will be no fine or other punishment.

"However if you despise the blood of my messenger, I will know that you choose to continue to despise me as well. Then I will send my warriors on you like locusts. If you reject me not once but twice, you will pay with your own blood, every last drop of it.

"The king has spoken. The medicine pouch is in your hands. What will you do with the blood of the messenger?"

Parable, Dr. Stan Nussbaum, Southern Africa

In Memory of Laurenti

He got sick in the night
By noon he was dead.
Agnes walked out of the hut.
She wailed her grief
over the Grumenti valley
to call her neighbors,
to follow a custom deep in her tribe,
to help the children cry.

Laurenti and Agnes were baptized.
They had been married in Serengeti Parish.
They would walk miles, hours
in the burning sun to Mass,
to greet, to be there for God.

By August first, Agnes has harvested
the cotton, the milo, the beans.
The final Eucharist.
The end—a beginning.

Agnes and the children are moving.
We'll pack the chickens first.
We make a stick cage and
we chase the chickens through the milo
around the house, over the grave,
under the pickup, and we laugh.
Cotton? We bundle up the leftovers,
the colored stuff, the future mattress
and put them up on the cab.
The dog? Paulo is giving his dog to a
neighbor, a friend, his buddy.
We pack everything, even the table.
Then we lower the end gate,

spread the altar cloth,
prepare ourselves,
and pray
with heart.

Agnes and the children and I
are the only Catholics,
but everyone enjoys blessing the grave
blessing each child, imposing hands
on the treasures, the truck,
the children.

Singing in the cool morning air.
We have a musical word in Swahili:
kumsindikiza.
It means "to take a friend
down the road a bit."
And we pray Laurenti
down the road a bit,
to heaven, to new life.
God is with you, Laurenti.

The sky is blue blue above
the morning sun,
orange with Serengeti dust.
The valley far off, like heaven.
The God of Life and Death,
the Creator of Light and Dark,
the Infinite Invisible was pleased
to take him by the hand.

The Mass is ended.
Let's do it. Let's get on with life.

Poem, Father Don Larmore, Serengeti, Tanzania

He Went Like a Bar of Soap

Zacharias, an elderly African catechist, was laid to rest after a long life of serving his church and the people of Kenya. Afterwards, as I was walking back with another catechist, she remarked, "We'll miss him. He went *ki-sabuni* (Swahili for "like a bar of soap"). Confused, I asked, "Like a bar of what?" She repeated, "*Ki-sabuni.* You know. In the house the bar of soap sits next to the basin, available morning, noon, and night to all—children, adults, the elderly, family, and guests alike. It never discriminates or complains of being used and reused. It is taken for granted as it slowly disappears, until someone exclaims, 'Gosh, the soap is gone!' Zacharias was that kind of man. I'm sure the God he served so well will grant him eternal rest."

True story, Father Gerry Nolf, M.Afr., Kenya,
"Missioner Tales" (Maryknoll, October, 1991)

A Day of Life and Death and New Life

Sunday morning on the Feast of the Baptism of Jesus the Lord. I wake up with energy and excitement. Today we will have four infant baptisms. First I will baptize Candida and later in the day I will baptize three babies in another part of the parish. By 8 A.M. I have gathered my Mass kit and other supplies and set off. My four-wheel drive pickup is smeared with mud as it plows through the thick, black soil. I feel happy that these four Tanzanian infants are following in the footsteps of Jesus Christ himself.

I have a warm friendship with Candida's parents, who are active Christians, and I often visit their home for friendly conversation and a pleasant meal. We are all really looking forward to Candida's baptism, since their previous daughter Josephina, who was named after me, died when she was only a year old.

Shortly before I reached their village, another friend, Manyera, meets me on the road. When I begin to speak enthusiastically about the baptism to take place, he says quietly, "Father, I'm sorry to have to tell you, but Candida died last Thursday. She took sick suddenly and we didn't have any special medicine."

I sit stunned. A day of new life has become a day of death for me. Manyera explains that Candida's parents took her to the nearby health center but it was too late. No one knows what caused her death. I grieve for my friends.

As I begin to celebrate the Eucharist with tears in my eyes, I tell the Christians that what was to have been a joyful baptismal celebration will now be a special Eucharist to pray for Candida, who would have been four-and-a-half-months old.

In my homily I say, "God gives and God takes away" and I quote one of my favorite lines from the French philosopher Gabriel Marcel: "Life is not a series of problems but a network of mysteries." Yes, little Candida's death is a mystery—as are the deaths each year of more than a million African children

under the age of one. We can't explain the "why" of God's plan.

After the Eucharist I can't stop thinking of little Candida as I pack up the holy oils, candle, and white cloth I would have used for her baptism. Then Alex, the young assistant catechist, says, "Father Joseph, I have some happy news for you. I have a new baby brother. My mother gave birth a week ago today."

I am overjoyed. First death, now new life. God gives. God takes away. God gives again. I rush down the aisle to shake hands with the proud father, Vedastus.

Before I leave, I visit the newborn baby named Haruni after his deceased grandfather. I pick him up with great joy. His mother beams. Like many newborn African babies, he has light skin, which will darken in a few months. Haruni's older brother, three-year-old Fabian, is very clever and speaks Swahili well. He turns to me and says, "This little baby is a foreigner [he means a white person], just like Father Joseph."

I also visit Elizabeth, Candida's mother, to give her *pole*, the Swahili word for "sympathy." We silently grieve together. A tear falls when I remember that Candida lies next to Josephina in the family plot.

At my next stop, we gather outside the home of Ibrahimu Mahende, the father of Joseph, one of the three baby boys to be baptized. I explain how the ordinary symbols of water, oil, a white garment, and a candle signify our new life in baptism, our entry into the mystery of Christ's death and resurrection. To explain the importance of the white garment put on the infants, I quote the African writer who said, "To the African, religion is like the skin you carry along with you wherever you are, not like the cloth that you wear now and discard the next moment." Joy fills the whole ceremony as we sing songs about happiness, hope, and new life. The women dance and wave leafy branches in front of the newly baptized children.

The joy of the baptismal ceremony lightens my spirits. Here is new life. A family member takes my picture holding little Joseph—we are namesakes. The whole day has been a journey into the mystery of life and death and new life. From Candida's sudden death to Haruni's joyful birth and the happiness of the baptisms of Joseph, James, and Paul. God gives. God takes away. God gives again. And again!

True story, Father Joseph Healey, M.M., Iramba, Tanzania,
"A Day of Life and Death and New Life," in
What Language Does God Speak:
African Stories about Christmas and Easter
(St. Paul Publications—Africa, 1989)

Enjoying a Safe Meal

While on the road to Nairobi, Kenya, a fellow missionary and I stopped for lunch in Nakuru. We had parked not far from a sidewalk vendor selling French-fried potatoes and other fried foods. When I approached the little stand, my horrified companion explained to me that such places were unsafe and cited a long list of diseases that can be contracted from unclean food. Overhearing his remark, the vendor assured us that his food was fresh and had not been left in old grease. But my friend disagreed, saying food that had obviously been left out for so long should be thrown out.

Just beyond the stand was a small restaurant. There we enjoyed a "safe" meal, including tasty French fries. As we returned to our truck we passed the vendor and noticed that he had cleaned out his stand.

"I'm glad to see you took my advice," said my friend, "and threw out that old food, including those greasy French-fried potatoes."

"Oh no," replied the vendor, "someone from the small restaurant next door just bought all my food a little while ago."

True story, Dan Griffin, MMAF, Nakuru, Kenya
"Missioner Tales" (Maryknoll)

No Food, Casimir

I am traveling in northern Tanzania on a paved road about thirty miles from Arusha. Suddenly I get a flat tire. After putting on the spare, I discover that it too is flat. I wave the next car to a stop and send a written message for help to the nearest gas station.

It is about one o'clock in the afternoon and the tropical sun is beating down on the semi-desert Maasailand. Except for the paved road there is only wilderness for miles in each direction.

After a few minutes, a young Maasai boy walks up. He is herding cattle. He tells me that his name is Casimir. He peers into the fully loaded car and examines all the boxes.

"Is it food?" he asks hopefully.

"No, only books."

Casimir is disappointed. He must be very hungry. All day long he sits in the glaring sun watching the cows graze on short tufts of grass and small bushes. Like many Maasai boys, he doesn't go to school. The nearest school is more than thirty miles away and there is also a tradition that Maasai boys should herd cattle as their fathers did. While I am waiting, numerous cars and buses go by. A white sedan races past. Then the driver abruptly hits the brakes. The car backs up and a cheerful Asian in his early thirties leans out the window and asks, "Do you need any help?"

"Thanks," I answer, "but I've already sent word for help to a garage in Arusha." With a wave of his hand, the driver sets off.

I relax in my seat and wonder about this friendly man who has just left. He stopped and wanted to help. Yet in many places in East Africa his presence (and that of other Asians) is no longer wanted.

A few minutes later Casimir's father, Leo, comes by. He is a tall, stately Moran (the name given to Maasai warriors) and is very curious about my car. He examines the outside carefully, tapping his walking stick against the door. After we talk briefly, he asks if he can sit inside.

For more than an hour Leo and I, sitting side by side in the front seat, discuss his large herd of cattle, the crops, and Casimir's future schooling. Then he says goodbye and walks off.

Almost three hours after I have sent word, a car from an Arusha garage drives up. We put on a good tire and I am ready to leave. By this time Casimir has told his shepherd friends about the *mguu mbovu* (Swahili for "bad tire"). So now four more herds of cattle munch grass in the adjoining field and five young Maasai boys watch them. I wave goodbye and drive off to Arusha. On the way I think of many things, but mainly of Casimir asking for food but finding only books.

True story, Father Joseph Healey, M.M., Arusha, Tanzania,
"No Food, Casimir" (Maryknoll, November, 1975)

Two Roads Overcame the Hyena

A very hungry hyena went out on the Tanzanian plains to hunt for food. He came to a fork in the road where two paths veered off in different directions. The hyena saw two goats caught in thickets, one at the end of each path. With his mouth watering in anticipation, he decided that his left leg would follow the left path and his right leg the right path. As the two paths grew farther apart, he kept trying to follow them both at once. Finally he split in two.

As the well-known African proverb says, "Two roads overcame the hyena."

Folktale, Tanzania

A Three-Year-Old Boy Challenged Me to Holiness

Today in Umtata, South Africa, a three-year-old boy challenged me to holiness.

I treated him for an earache when he was brought in by a neighbor. She showed me the marks on his body and back. Red raised welts covered this fragile little body, but his face was expressionless as I groaned in pain at the sight. "Nothing new, that's life," the look on the woman's face seemed to say. As some sort of gesture of kindness, I gave him a sweet.

Next patient. Another little boy covered in scabies (tiny bugs that get under the skin and cause an itchy rash). I prepared the treatment, and out of the corner of my eye I saw the first little boy give half of his precious sweet to this second boy. Without a thought and completely on his own.

This boy touched my soul and humbled me to the core. He had done what I only hope to do.

True story, Heidi Schmidt, Umtata, South Africa

How Fast You Carry the Flashlight

Heading into the game park in Tanzania on his first safari, the American visitor was confident that he could handle any emergency. He sidled up to the experienced local guide and said smugly, "I know that carrying a flashlight will keep the lions away."

"True," the guide replied, "but it depends on how fast you carry the flashlight."

True story, Tanzania,
collected by Father Joseph Healey, M.M

Family

"I belong by blood relationship; therefore I am."
Akan proverb from Ghana

The African emphasis on the importance of personal relationships is closely connected to the African understanding of family. Whether part of the immediate family or the extended family or simply close friends or even visitors, everyone participates in the family's relationships and friendships. These relationships develop within the ever-widening circles of the nuclear family, the normal extended family, the larger extended family of blood relationships, the clan, and the ethnic group. When two young Africans marry, then, the marriage is not just a contract between two individuals, but is rather a bond or covenant between two large extended families.

The term "family" is often used by African Christians to describe the church. All people in the world are sons and daughters of God. They are bound together in a worldwide family of past, present, and future generations, a family that incorporates all races and all ethnic groups. In this great extended family of God, God the Father is the "Chief Ancestor," Jesus Christ is the "Eldest Brother," and Christian ancestors are the saints.

Within the family, elders are greatly respected and their advice is regularly sought and followed. Severe hardships and great joys are equally shared, along with resources, whether abundant, adequate, or meager. Marriages are celebrated, as are newly born children, who are then nurtured and watched over by the entire community. This is reflected in the well-known West African proverb, "It takes a whole village to raise a child."

I Carry My Brother

On a steep and rocky path in Africa, I encountered a small girl who carried on her back her little brother. "My child," I said to her, "you carry a heavy burden."

She looked at me and said: "I carry not a heavy burden. I carry my brother!" I was speechless.

The words of this child sank deep into my heart. When people's troubles seem to weigh me down to a point where I nearly lose heart, the words of the child come back to me: "I carry not a heavy burden. I carry my brother!"

Parable, Africa, quoted by Marc Sevin,
"Editorial" (Bulletin Dei Verbum, *25, 1993*)

Giving Food to Your Children That You Won't Eat Yourself

Katarataro, one of my neighbors who belonged to an African religion, asked for baptism for his newborn twins. Clearly, he wanted the "power" of Christian names to protect his children from evil spirits.

In refusing him, a visiting bishop shrewdly drew a comparison with African family traditions. Parents, he said, always make sure to sample the food before giving it to their children. The mother especially checks the taste or flavor of all the food.

Comparing the Christian life to food, the bishop asked Katarataro, "Would you give food to your children that you won't eat yourself?"

Katarataro had no answer to the bishop's question. He walked away sad, but with plenty to think about.

True story, Father Joseph Healey, M.M., Nyabihanga, Tanzania,
A Fifth Gospel: The Experience of Black Christian Values
(Orbis Books, 1981)

The Dying Father's Last Testament to His Three Sons

There was an old man who lived with his wife and their three beloved sons. After getting very sick and realizing that he had only a few days left here on earth, he started to give his three sons special advice about their future life. First, the father insisted on the importance of his children staying in close contact with the people in their clan, such as, for example, their aunts and uncles.

Then, two days before his death, he called his children into the room where he was lying in bed and said: "My sons, I ask each of you to go outside and bring back one stick."

The three children did as they were asked. Then the old man asked his eldest son to break his stick. He bent it and broke it. Then the father asked his second and third sons to do the same. They each successfully broke their sticks.

Next, the old man asked his three sons to go out again and get similar sticks. When they returned, he asked his eldest son to tie the three sticks together in a bundle. Then he asked his firstborn son to try to break the three sticks as he had done earlier with his one stick. But he could not break the bundle of three sticks together. The second son also tried but failed. So too the third son.

Finally, the old man gave his last testament to his three children by saying: "It is important for you to always stay together like this bundle of sticks. 'Unity is strength. Division is weakness.'"

True story, Sukuma ethnic group,
Joseph Lupande, Bujora, Tanzania

The Dead Are Never Dead

Those who are dead have never gone away.
They are in the shadows darkening around,
They are in the shadows fading into day,
The dead are not under the ground.
They are in the trees that quiver,
They are in the woods that weep,
They are in the waters of the rivers,
They are in the waters that sleep.
They are in the crowds,
They are in the homestead.
The dead are never dead.

Poem, Africa,
Birago Diop, A Book of African Verse
(Heinemann, 1964)

Amazed at Her Ingenuity

While walking home from a leadership workshop in Kenya's Chalbi Desert, I caught up to five-year-old Sori. She was knitting, her tiny fingers flying as she walked to the local shop to buy sugar. Admiring handiwork done by one so young, I asked what she was going to do with her yet-small piece of cloth. "It's a blanket to protect my new baby brother from the cold desert wind at night," she replied.

Impressed, I was even more amazed at her ingenuity. Her knitting needles were four-inch thorns cut from trees surrounding her settlement.

True story, Sister Jacqueline Dorr, M.M., Chalbi Desert, Kenya

The Two Brothers

Two brothers wanted to go to a distant country to make their fortune. They asked their father for a blessing, saying, "Father, we are going away to make our fortune. May we have your blessing, please?"

Their father agreed. "Go with my blessing, but on your way put marks on the trees lest you get lost."

After they received the blessing, the two brothers set off on their safari. The older brother entered the forest and, as he made his way through it, cut down some of the trees and made marks on other trees. He did this for the whole length of his journey.

The younger brother took another route. As he was walking along, he came to a house. He knocked on the door, was invited in, and made friends with the children of that family. He stayed there for a while and then continued along on his way, making friends through the whole length of his journey.

Finally, the two brothers returned home. Their father gave them a warm welcome, saying, "How happy I am to see you back home again, my sons, especially since you have returned safely. Wonderful! Now I would like to see the marks that you have left on the trees."

So the father went off with his first-born son. On the way, the son showed his father all the trees that he had cut down and others he had marked along the way. They traveled a long distance without eating and finally returned home empty-handed, as they had set out.

Next, the father set out with his second-born son. During the journey, various friends warmly received the younger son and his father, who were treated as special guests at each place they visited, with goats often slaughtered to prepare a feast to welcome them. When the father and his son returned home, they brought with them many gifts they had received.

Then the father summoned his two sons and said, "Dear sons, I have seen the work that you have done. I will arrange a marriage for the one who has done better."

He turned to the first-born son and said, "My son, I think you are foolish. You do not know how to take care of people. I told you to put marks on the trees wherever you passed, but you have cut down many trees. Where is the profit in all these felled trees?"

Turning to the second son, he said, "My son, you are clever. I am happy you have left such important marks on your journey. Wherever we passed, we received a fine welcome. This came from your good relationships with the people we visited."

Then he said, "My dear children, now it is time for me to give my reward. I am going to arrange a big feast for my younger son. We will slaughter a cow for him, for my younger son has left good and lasting marks wherever he passed."

True story, Sukuma ethnic group, Tanzania,
collected by the Sukuma Research Committee, Bujora, Tanzania

No Food for Her Children

The mother in Torit, Sudan, has no food left for her children. The pots in her hut are empty, but only she knows this. The children just trust Mama. They don't know they are poor.

She tells the children she is going to cook, but that it will be troublesome if they are all around when she unpacks the dried meat from the pot at the back. So the children are sent outside.

The meat pot is empty. She fills the cooking pot with stones and water and puts it on the fire. Then she calls the children back in and asks them to keep the fire going. Dried meat takes a long time to cook, and the children, thinking they are cooking meat, forget all about being hungry.

The mother goes into the woods to find food, but, as many others have discovered, there is little remaining there. The basket on her head stays empty, and she is desperate.

Suddenly, she hears a lion roar nearby. She is frightened to death of lions, yet she draws closer to the sound and, from behind a tree, she watches the lion devouring a buffalo. Oh, she is afraid, but she also knows that the meat will keep her children alive.

She takes the circlet of grass, with which she balances her basket, from her head and flings it at the lion to divert its attention. It works. When the lion pounces on the grass ring, the mother throws sand on the buffalo meat, knowing that lions do not eat soiled flesh. When the lion returns, it recoils from its meal. The mother fills her basket with the soiled flesh, goes to wash it in the river, and runs home.

The children are still minding the fire. She sends them out again and quickly cooks the fresh meat, which does not take long. Her children and those of the neighbors have something to eat that day.

Only the mother knows how close all of them had been to starvation.

True story, Bishop Paride Taban, Torit, Sudan in Matthew Haumann,
The Long Road to Peace: Encounters with the People of Southern Sudan
(Gracewing, 2000)

So God Has to Be Both

Some years ago I was getting a haircut in the district town of Maswa, Tanzania. When I told the barber that I was flying to the United States, he asked me about some of the topics that Americans talk about and even disagree on. I mentioned the controversy over whether God should be called both Father and Mother, or Father only.

The barber commented: "That's an easy question. We are children of God. To give birth to children you need a Father and a Mother. So God has to be both."

True story, Father Joseph Healey, M.M., Maswa, Tanzania

Veronica Gives Birth to a Boy Child

On December 23rd I was returning from an outlying village with several people riding in my pick-up truck. Transportation is scarce on the rough, dirt roads of Tanzania. The only option is usually a long, tiring walk in the boiling African sun. The local people often say that giving "lifts" is one of the most valuable services a priest provides!

An obviously pregnant young woman standing by the side of the road signaled for a lift. She wanted to get to the closest health center. The other passengers insisted that she sit in front with me. "She is with child," they said. Their happy faces spoke to me of how highly Africans value life. Their expressions seemed to say: "She will soon give birth. Children are life. Children are hope. Children are the future."

As we drove, we talked. Her name was Veronica. Shy at first—part of the African tradition of a woman hesitating to talk to a stranger—she explained that her first pregnancy had been difficult. Her husband had wanted a boy, but she had given birth to a girl. "It's all in God's plan," Veronica said, but this time she wanted a boy to carry on the family line, so important in the African tradition.

As we jolted along a particularly rough section of the road, we fell silent. She couldn't have been more than twenty years old, but she was a busy mother, housewife, farmer, and general provider. Such is the typical life of women in rural Africa. She was poor but she radiated joy and happiness, undoubtedly due in large part to the anticipation of giving birth. If a vehicle hadn't come along, she likely would have started the journey of ten miles on foot. I thought of another woman who had been pregnant with child and had made a similar journey almost two thousand years before.

Veronica sheepishly admitted that she was a Catholic but not much of a churchgoer. "I'm always so busy," she said. But she said that she knew Christmas would be coming in two days and that it would be a great celebration.

When I commented that she was very special, she looked at me with surprise and asked, "Why is that, Padri? I'm just an ordinary woman."

I explained that she would give birth around Christmas, reminding us of when Mary gave birth to Jesus in a stable in Bethlehem. As Veronica listened wide-eyed, I recounted the story of the first Christmas, emphasizing the tender and loving role of Mary. I ended by saying, "And this birth changed the whole world."

When the rough ride was over, she said, "I really don't know much about the Christmas story, but this year I'll remember what you have told me." Then, with downcast eyes, she said, "But this year I won't be able to go to church on Christmas."

"Don't worry," I told her. "The most important thing is that you give birth safely. Think of Mary and Jesus as you lie on your bed in the health center."

"I will," exclaimed Veronica. "Oh, yes, I will."

On Christmas Eve I made the five-minute walk to the health center to see how Veronica was doing. Both she and Mary were close to delivery time. I blessed Veronica and prayed for a safe delivery. Then I hurried back to the church to make sure everything was ready for our midnight Mass.

On Christmas day I left very early to celebrate the Christmas liturgy at two distant churches and returned in the late afternoon. A few minutes after I had gotten back, I heard a knock at the door and a woman's voice say *"Hodi, Padri"* ("I'm here, Father" in Swahili). A beaming Veronica was holding her newborn baby. I felt like the first Christmas story was unfolding in front of me.

After giving birth, African mothers are often on their feet the same day or the next, but seeing Veronica was like a miracle. She exclaimed, "It's a boy, just like we hoped! My husband will be so happy." She continued, "I had a difficult time last night, but I gave birth at about eleven o'clock. According to what you told me, that's very close to the time when the Blessed Virgin Mary gave birth to Jesus."

The joy on Veronica's face communicated much more than words. We talked for a few minutes and then parted. My only thought was "God is good. Oh, yes, God is good. Two thousand years ago, in Bethlehem, Mary gave birth to a boy child. Last night, right here, Veronica also gave birth to a boy child."

True story, Father Joseph Healey, M.M., Iramba, Tanzania,
"Veronica Gives Birth to a Boy Child," in
What Language Does God Speak:
African Stories about Christmas and Easter
(*St. Paul Publications–Africa, 1989*)

Your Mother Wants to Greet You

When I returned to my parish in Tanzania after a journey to the United States because of my mother's serious sickness and death, the local Christians gave me plenty of *pole*, the Swahili equivalent of sympathy or condolence. My good friends Robert and Maria, at whose marriage I had officiated, came to express sympathy and show me their new baby, born when I was away.

"*Padri*," Thomas said, "in our African tradition, when a person dies, he or she does not just disappear but remains part of our community. We often name the next child after the deceased to preserve this ongoing memory. We want to baptize our newborn girl with the name of Virginia to continue your mother's presence among us."

At that moment, Maria put little Virginia into my arms and said, "Your mother wants to greet you." Tears came to my eyes, but I was very happy.

True story, Father Joseph Healey, M.M., Iramba, Tanzania

Nothing Materially but Everything Spiritually

In Shinyanga, Tanzania, we visited some friends of my Uncle Ernie, a Maryknoll priest. They were a husband and wife with leprosy who had been eventually cured with the help of Uncle Ernie and some patrons back home. They had built a large, very neat home, creating an oasis in the middle of nowhere full of banana trees, mangos, rice, and many other crops.

What was most beautiful, however, was this family. They had four children, none with leprosy. Each was a delight. The oldest daughter, Rebecca, was married to George and had a beautiful little baby. Since the baby had been born healthy, George's father agreed to pay the dowry for Rebecca. This was a great financial boost to her family.

Before dinner the whole family knelt in the dust to pray the rosary and to thank God for his bounty. As an American, I found this to be remarkable. The parents had no fingers or toes left and had otherwise been disfigured by their leprosy. They could have cursed God for their afflictions, but instead they held their rosaries between the nubs that had been fingers, knelt in the dirt in front of their mud hut, and thanked God for their many blessings. It was beautiful and humbling and amazing all at once.

Afterwards, as I helped them pound the husks off the rice and watched the chaff blowing in the wind, I couldn't help but admire these simple people—they had nothing materially but everything spiritually. I realized that eventually I would be returning to witness more true poverty in America than I had seen in any part of Tanzania.

True story, Paul Nadeau, Shinyanga, Tanzania

Community

"When spider webs unite, they can tie up a lion."
Amharic proverb from Ethiopia

In African society, a person is first and foremost a member of the community and second an individual. A person's life, therefore, is to be focused on the well-being of the community. This is summed up in one of the most significant African proverbs: "I am because we are; we are because I am." Traditionally, whatever happens to the individual happens to the whole community and whatever happens to the whole community happens to the individual.

Despite this traditional emphasis on community values, many Africans struggle with living out these values in contemporary society. In particular, the economic pressures of life in the fast-growing, sprawling African cities present a challenge. A core traditional value in Africa, for example, is participation, rather than achievement. If a person's community is distant or diffuse, how can a person participate, contribute, and share? Yet, without personal achievement, how can one survive in the city?

One particular sign of the times in the church in Africa today is the rapid growth of small Christian communities. For African Christians, these groups usually reflect the traditional values of African community: those of participation, consensus, and solidarity. Such small communities support African Christians who desire to maintain traditional values rather than be absorbed into individualism or materialism. This new way of "being church" has much to teach urban dwellers in the West who seek a greater meaning in life than a bigger house or better car.

Padri, Why Are You Trying to Break Us Up?

When I served as a priest in Tanzania, I spent a year preparing a group of Maasai for baptism. I had to decide who seemed ready and who needed more study.

Ndangoya, the oldest man, stopped me politely but firmly. "*Padri*, why are you trying to break us up and separate us? During this whole year you have been teaching us. We have talked about these things when you were not here, at night around the fire. Yes, there have been lazy ones in this community. But they have been helped by those with much energy. There are stupid ones in the community, but they have been helped by those who are intelligent. There are ones with little faith in this village, but they have been helped by those with much faith. Would you turn out and drive off those lazy ones and the ones with little faith and the stupid ones? From the first day, I have spoken for these people—and I still speak for them. Now, on this day one year later, I can declare for them and for all this community that we have reached the step in our lives where we can say, 'We believe.'"

I looked at the old man. "Excuse me, old man," I said. "Sometimes my head is hard and I learn slowly. 'We believe,' you said. Of course you do. Everyone in the community will be baptized."

True story, Father Vincent Donovan, C.S.S.P., Arusha, Tanzania,
Christianity Rediscovered *(Orbis, 2002)*

Two Villages

There once were two villages separated by a river. In one of these villages lived RraSephiri (Mr. Secret). RraSephiri was the only one in his village who knew how to make chairs. He carefully guarded his secret way of making chairs. He was afraid to teach others because he thought that they would not make the chairs correctly.

Over time, all the chairs in the village were built by RraSephiri, but he still worried. What if someone found out his secret? What if someone else came to the village to show people how to make such nice chairs? He grew to be suspicious of people. If he saw anyone with some wood, he feared that they might be making a chair. He would ridicule them and warn them not to try to make a chair themselves.

People in the village gradually became unhappy and frightened. They stayed away from RraSephiri. They still went to him for chairs, but they did not like to be near him for long. While the young people wanted to work with RraSephiri, they were too afraid of him to ask. He never shared his secret with them and eventually some of them even left the village.

In the village across the river there lived a man named RraMosupatsela (Mr. Guide). He also knew how to build very good chairs. But RraMosupatsela did not keep his knowledge a

secret. He wanted others to learn how to build chairs as he did. So, he told everyone who came to him exactly how he built such nice chairs and where to get the wood.

Soon the younger men in the village were also making chairs. Sometimes one of them would discover a new way to improve the chair. He would show RraMosupatsela and then RraMosupatsela would tell him to show the others. In this way, the chairs in this village kept getting better and better. People from other villages would come to watch as RraMosupatsela and his young men worked under the big morula tree. They laughed and told stories as they worked together.

When people praised RraMosupatsela's chairs, he would laugh and say, "I did not build these chairs alone. These young men have improved my chairs. I am getting old, but these young men will continue building better and better chairs. I have given my skills and knowledge to them and they have given their love and friendship to me. Together we have done far more than if I had worked alone."

Parable, Southern Africa,
Rudy Dirks, Gaborone, Botswana,
"Nussbaum Awards"
(The Review of AICs, *January–April, 2001*)

Adaka, the Old Man

An old man named Adaka spent most of his day sitting on the verandah of his mud hut, smoking his pipe. His village in Malawi had fertile land and hard-working people. Adaka was well known and many people exchanged words with him as they passed by.

One day, as Adaka watched a stream of strangers coming into the village for the annual harvest festival, a young man who had a spring in his steps and a ready smile approached him and said, "Excuse me, old man, but I have left my village where there is starvation and I am looking for a place where I can cultivate some fields and settle. I would like to ask your advice. Are the people of this village good and are they ready to welcome a stranger?"

Adaka took a long draw from his pipe and asked, "How are the people in the village you left?"

"Well," answered the young man, "they are good. They solve their quarrels with the mediation of the elders and they work together when there is a need. The evenings of feastdays are wonderful. I get homesick when I think about them. And the girls —they are certainly the most beautiful and tender to be found."

Adaka smiled and said, "Do not worry, young man. The people in this village are as good as those you have left."

The young man went on with a determined gait and after a few minutes he was lost in the market crowd.

After a while, another young man arrived. He looked around suspiciously, appraised Adaka with a long look, and then approached him and said, "I would like to settle in this place, but how are the people?"

Adaka took a long time to refill his pipe. He then asked, "How are the people in the village you left?"

The young man answered with a sneer, "Bad! They are envious and jealous. They never recognized my talent. I am so glad I left them."

Adaka's face took on a worried look and he slowly said, "Then you had better not even enter this village. Here people are exactly as those you have left behind. You will not find any friends here."

The young man turned away in disgust.

Adaka's granddaughter, who was nearby grinding corn, overheard the conversation of her grandfather with the passersby. She waited for the second young man to leave and then said to Adaka in an astonished voice, "But Grandfather, you have cheated one of the two boys! You gave completely different answers to the same question."

Adaka explained. "You see, people are to us what we want them to be. If we treat them with kindness and consideration, they will become our friends. If we despise them, they will despise us in turn. The first young man will find friends everywhere he goes. The second will make enemies everywhere, as that is what he imagines those he encounters to be. The difference is not in my answers, but in their hearts."

Parable, Father Renato Kizito Sesana, MCCJ, Malawi,
"The Sin of Conformity"
(New People Feature Service, *15 February, 1999*)

The Human Mirrors of Community

One afternoon I was returning to my home from a village in Sierra Leone. I had my little red backpack flung over my shoulder. The children knew that I often had my camera in that backpack. As I walked down the path, I noticed some little children up in a mango tree. I couldn't really see them, but I could hear them calling, "Anita, Anita, come snap we!"

When I walked to the tree and saw those smiling faces looking down at me, I thought this would make a great photo. So I snapped straight up into the tree.

I sent the film home to my brother who mailed back a copy of the photo for each of the children. Word soon spread in the village, "The photos are in, the photos are in!"

Little Mohammed eagerly led his mother to my home and asked, "Anita, Anita, you get the photos?"

I answered, "Yes, Mohammed, I get the photos."

As he looked at the snapshot, he identified each of his little friends. But he did not name himself. Pointing, his mother said gently, "Mohammed, this now you."

I realized that, because in this village there are no mirrors as we know them, little Mohammed did not recognize his own face! Mohammed knew himself only through his mother, his friends, and other neighbors. The people of this village saw themselves through human mirrors. When they greeted each other, "How are you today?" or when they said, "I'm sorry that you're sick," or "That's not a good thing you're doing," they learned about who they were.

I prayed that night, asking God, "If modern mirrors ever come to this village, please don't let the people here lose their human mirrors."

True story, Anita Kennedy, VMM, Sierra Leone,
"The Mirrors of Community"
(Buena Vista Ink, *January–February, 1997*)

The Two Young Men on the Road to Nakuru

One day, two young men were on their way back to their home village. John and Charles had gotten on the bus in Nairobi. On their journey they began talking about all the problems they had encountered in Nairobi in the previous six months. Like many rural Kenyan youth, they had left their village before finishing high school and traveled to Nairobi to find jobs. It took some time, but John got a job washing dishes in a small restaurant and Charles, a good handyman, got occasional work as a day laborer in an outdoor garage. It was not much, but it was a start.

They joined a group of young men connected to the "Movement for a New Kenya," one of the main opposition parties that spoke out against bribery and corruption in the government. John and Charles volunteered a lot of their free time and often participated in protest rallies. They enjoyed the ferment of the big city, but they realized that things were getting more dangerous in Kenya.

Then everything started to go wrong. One day there was a big riot in downtown Nairobi after a political rally they had attended. Three people were killed and the party's leader was arrested as an enemy of the state. Their hopes for a "New Kenya" were dashed.

To make matters worse, John's picture appeared as part of the story in one of the daily newspapers. When his boss heard about it, John was immediately fired. Then their small flat was broken into and they lost most of their belongings. And after Charles missed work three times because he was ill with malaria, the garage let him go.

John and Charles grew very disillusioned with life in the big city of Nairobi. Everything was so expensive. When their money finally ran out, they decided to take a bus back to their village.

A man in his mid-thirties had been reading a book in the next seat while John and Charles had been conversing on the bus. When the bus stopped because of a flat tire, John and Charles struck up a conversation with the man and began telling him all their troubles. They talked about their political activity and how they had given up the traditions of their people for the fast Western lifestyle of Nairobi. They expressed their disappointment at their failure.

The stranger said he was a lawyer and asked them about their commitment to bring about social change in Kenya. Were they ready to make real sacrifices to promote justice and peace? Why had they given up their African customs to follow the latest foreign music and clothes styles? The lawyer said that, instead of listening to fast-talking politicians and their many promises, it would be better to work for change from the grassroots and to be a "voice for the voiceless." Were they really interested in serving others or only in satisfying themselves?

Later, when they stopped for lunch, John and Charles urged the lawyer to have lunch with them. He said that he had studied African traditions very carefully and that African customs, sayings, and stories contain a lot of wisdom for the world today. He talked about the African custom of sharing a meal, commenting on the fact that fast-food restaurants destroy the value of eating together. A meal is perhaps the most basic and ancient symbol of friendship, love, and unity, he said. Food and drink taken in common are signs of shared life. The stranger used the African proverb "Relationship is in the eating together" to explain how a pleasant meal that is shared can build community and trust. He talked about the human and spiritual values of sharing.

Then the man called over the waiter, paid the bill, and, with a quick wave, left. The two youths sat amazed. Now he was gone. Who was he? Then they recalled a famous and outspoken civil rights lawyer who had been living in exile in England and who always championed the poor and victimized. Could it have been he?

During the rest of the journey, John and Charles talked. They decided to continue on to their home village with new hope and purpose to make a fresh start. Perhaps later they might return to Nairobi and help bring about real change in Kenya.

Parable, Father Joseph Healey, M.M., Nairobi, Kenya,
"The Two Young Men on the Road to Nakuru," in
Towards an African Narrative Theology *(Orbis Books, 1996)*

The Redemptive Power of Love

Anton used to work for the Tanzanian government, pushing heavy carts of supplies around the city of Musoma. He often took supplies to Nyabangi, the local camp for lepers. For years he was abusive and cruel to the lepers there. Mamy years later, Anton got sick. He had no family to support him, and so he became a ward of the government. Now, stripped of his strength, he had to take his place among the neglected poor. He was sent to Nyabangi to live among the very people he had abused, to live like them, as one who was completely dependent on others for his care.

Last week Anton died. At his funeral there was no one from his family, no one from the government, only the people who had loved and cared for him through his last, most desperate years—the lepers of Nyabangi. As they buried Anton, I saw their grief. It wasn't merely a case of poetic justice. I saw the redemptive power of love.

True story, Dan Griffin, MMAF, Nyabangi, Tanzania

On the Way to Bauleni

Two Zambian bishops returned to Lusaka from Rome after the 1994 African Synod of Bishops. They resembled the disciples returning to Emmaus. They were tired, disappointed, disillusioned, and even depressed about their month of hard work in Rome and the uncertain results of their efforts.

Shortly after their return to Africa, a taxi driver named Mtonga took them to the meeting of a small Christian community in an area known as Bauleni, a squatter neighborhood. A young woman with a two-week-old baby, a young man with the dreams of youth, and an elderly refugee spoke with the bishops.

As the bishops listened, their hearts were deeply moved. They had been bored while listening to the solemn speeches given in the Vatican hall during the synod. And now, the simple language of their people set their hearts on fire. Their tiredness was gone. Their spirits were renewed.

The lay Christians had ministered to the two bishops and given them new hope. The younger bishop said, "They have proclaimed the Resurrected Lord to us."

Parable, Father Renato Kizito Sesana, MCCJ, Lusaka, Zambia

Good Times and Bad Times

"After hardship comes relief."
Swahili proverb from Eastern and Central Africa

An apt description of Africa today is "the good news in a bad-news situation." The continent has enormous problems. Every day eighty-five hundred people die from AIDS. In sub-Saharan Africa HIV/AIDS now kills more people than war. By the end of 2002, seventeen million people had died of AIDS—over three times the number of AIDS deaths in the rest of the world. Today thirty million Africans are living with HIV and approximately 95 percent of all AIDS orphans in the world live in sub-Saharan Africa. Given these statistics, it's difficult to realize that only 1.6 percent of world funding for scientific research against AIDS is allocated to Africa.

At present, nineteen of the fifty-three independent countries in Africa are presently undergoing some form of civil war or ethnic conflict. With so much fighting, warfare is all that many young Africans have known, and they think that it is normal, the way life is. This situation has resulted in more than four million refugees, almost one-quarter of the world's total, with an estimated fifteen million internally displaced persons.

Church workers and other humanitarian workers feel called to accompany the local people in these difficulties and, where they can, try to make a small difference. For them, and for the African people, life is filled with paradox: joy and sadness, success and failure, rising and falling and rising again. Meanwhile, we try to live out the words of Luke's Gospel, "To bring good news to the poor, to proclaim release to the captives and recovery of sight to the blind, to let the oppressed go free, to proclaim the year of the Lord's favor."

The African people give us a reason and hope for being there. The values they place on personal relationships, hospitality, sharing, patient endurance in adversity, sacrifice, and service to others teach us a great deal. This is the "good news" from Africa that motivates me to gather these stories. In the words of a Ganda proverb from Uganda, "One who sees something good must narrate it."

The Merciful Rwandan Wife

In a particular section of Kigali, Rwanda, where people from the Hutu and Tutsi ethnic groups lived together, the genocidal war broke out with a bloody vengeance. Neighbors attacked neighbors. In one area, a Hutu man murdered his Tutsi neighbor.

Some time later, after the Rwandan Patriotic Front had won the war and taken over the government, local investigations of the atrocities started. The wife of the dead Tutsi man was asked to identify her husband's murderer. She refused, knowing that the Hutu man would be arrested, imprisoned, and perhaps killed. The woman preferred to remain silent to save another life.

"This is enough" she said. "The killing has to stop somewhere. One murder does not justify another killing. We have to break the cycle of violence and end this genocide."

So she chose to forgive.

True story, told to Father Thomas McDonnell, M.M., Kigali, Rwanda

She Walked Like a Queen

My own fears of death are very present. I often think what it would be like if tomorrow I were told that I have cancer. Every day I have to tell people that they have AIDS, and some of them are very young.

I remember a young man who came to my office in Dar es Salaam recently to talk to Dorothy, the assistant medical director. Quietly I said to her, "Dorothy, he's coming to say goodbye."

I also remember a woman who came and said, "I want to go and see my mother."

I asked, "Do you think you are getting worse?"

"Yes, I think I am."

"Are you afraid?" I asked.

She replied, "No, I've done everything I want to do. My children are all right. I've made sure of that. But I do need to see my mother."

I gave her a hug. We said goodbye and I watched her walk up the street. Another counselor who had also said goodbye to her was watching with me.

The young woman walked like a queen. What she left in her wake was holy ground.

Video interview,
Sister Dr. Brigid Corrigan, M.M.M., M.D.,
Dar es Salaam, Tanzania,
Coming to Say Goodbye *(Maryknoll Productions, 2002)*

Schoolgirls Teach a Lesson of Love

On April 29, 1994, twenty-two people, mostly schoolgirls, were killed in an attack on a Catholic girls' school in Muramba in the Gisenyi Region of Rwanda near the border with the Democratic Republic of the Congo (formerly Zaire). During the genocidal war between Hutu and Tutsi, a group of armed men broke into the school and ordered the children to divide up into ethnic groups, Hutus on one side, Tutsi on the other. Witnessing to the fact that they were one loving community, the schoolgirls refused.

The men ruthlessly opened fire, killing seventeen girls and wounding fourteen. A Belgian missionary nun, Sister Margarita Bosmans, the directress of another school nearby who tried to stop the assassins, was also killed, along with four lay people.

True story, Muramba, Rwanda, based on the article,
"African Children Teach Us a Lesson of Love"
(The Seed, June 1997)

Otherwise This War Will Never End

This year we had an outbreak of meningitis. Biachirike hobbled into the hut unable to move her head. She was the oldest person to be stricken and had walked four days from her home to the refugee camp because of the war in southern Sudan. She had failed to get vaccine because she was building her house. I took her to the mud and grass "hospital" and asked the medical assistant to do a spinal tap. A bit of confusion ensued as she, a member of the Latuho ethnic group, asked what this Dinka man was going to do to her.

The Dinka nurse told her, "Mama, we are all your children and couldn't hurt you." She accepted this and acquiesced to the procedure, which confirmed that she had meningitis.

After two weeks of treatment, she was ready to go home. I reminded her of her question to "that Dinka man" and pointed out that he had saved her life.

One of the nurses added, "This hospital is like a church. When people come here, we don't notice their ethnic group, only that they are sick." The old woman shook my hand and headed for the door. Three Dinka women called out to her, begging her to say goodbye to them, too. As she shook each person's hand, I hoped that the next time they meet they would "remember" they are sisters and brothers.

Otherwise, this war will never end.

True story, Dr. Susan Nagele, MMAF, Southern Sudan

We Need to Run Out and Meet Lucia

St. Charles Lwanga small Christian community in Bunda, Tanzania, has special concern for the increasing number of people with AIDS. Martina Chacha, one of its leaders, is responsible for the ministry of "Good Neighbor." She regularly checks on the sick.

During the previous week, Maria Magesa's daughter, Lucia, had returned to Bunda after having spent more than two months in the tuberculosis ward of a nearby hospital. Lucia has AIDS and is now too weak to get out of bed. Although the family has been too embarrassed to tell anyone, word has slowly gotten around.

Martina has told the leaders in the Christian community about Lucia. At their next meeting, the Parable of the Prodigal Son is read and reflected upon. Someone points out that the father in the story does not wait for his younger son to return. Instead, he runs out to meet him. This is like God's great love for us. God is ready to run out to meet us in love, forgiveness, and compassionate care.

It is immediately clear what the community should do. As an elderly man puts it, "We need to run out and meet Lucia who is suffering."

After the meeting, everyone walks over to Maria Magesa's home to visit Lucia. It is dark inside the small bedroom. Lucia has no husband, which is increasingly common these days. Her two young children are sitting quietly in the corner. Lucia herself is lying on her side in bed, too weak to sit up. Her face is drawn and flushed. Her arms are thin and bony.

Martina Chacha quietly sits down on the bed, takes Lucia's hand, and tells her how much the small community members care about her. One man explains how suffering can be a special call from God. After prayers of intercession, everyone—even the children—lays hands on Lucia to pray for her recovery. Then

they give her mother a small donation of flour and money. Then there is a painful moment of silence. Everyone realizes how many families in the area have a loved one who is either sick with AIDS or who has already died. Many people, like Lucia, come home to die. The disease is ravishing East Africa, especially on the other side of Lake Victoria and up into western Uganda. AIDS has no favorites. Rich and poor, old and young, educated and uneducated, city and rural people alike are getting AIDS or are HIV-positive.

Most families try to hide the existence of AIDS. The shame is too great. Most people in Africa get AIDS from multi-partner heterosexual relationships, and people don't want to be confronted with questions about their personal lifestyles. Others pass it off as "just another illness." Still others say that it is "simply bad luck" or that they are "bewitched."

As they walk out of Lucia's dark room, temporarily blinded by the bright African sunlight, the small community members all wonder if and when they will see Lucia again.

In talking about people with AIDS, Blessed Teresa of Calcutta once said, "Today people with AIDS are the most unwanted and unloved brothers and sisters of Jesus. So let us give them our tender love and care and a beautiful smile."

The ministry of love and compassion to Lucia and many like her will continue. This is what Christianity is all about.

Historical fiction story,
Father Joseph Healey, M.M., Musoma, Tanzania

President Nyerere Disguises Himself as a Beggar

In 1974 Tanzania had a serious famine. The government provided famine relief, but the food was not getting to the people, so they complained to the authorities. The president of Tanzania, Julius Nyerere, heard about the complaints and decided to visit storehouses of the National Milling Company where the food was being kept.

He disguised himself as a beggar wearing worn-out clothes and an old hat. When he arrived at the main warehouse gate, no one recognized him. He passed through without permission and went straight to the office of the manager. He knocked on the door and yelled out, "Hey, you people in there! Help me. I don't have any food."

The manager answered, "Stop bothering us, old man. We don't have any food here. Go to the market and buy some for yourself." As the African proverb says, "A satisfied person does not know the hungry person."

Nyerere continued to cry out, but no one paid attention. The manager and his assistant were busy with some local businessmen who were buying the famine relief food that was supposed to go to the Tanzanian people. Finally, Nyerere opened the door and walked into the office. He took off his hat and made himself known. Needless to say, the manager was speechless.

After President Nyerere returned to Dar es Salaam, it was announced that the manager of the company had been fired together with some of his assistants.

True story, Father Donald Sybertz, M.M.
"President Nyerere Disguises Himself as a Beggar"
(Maryknoll Fathers and Brothers
Africa Region Newsletter, *August 2003*)

The Short Lives of Emmanuel and John

On December 23rd, Aurelia, the first wife of Nchabukoroka, gave birth to twin boys two homesteads away from where I lived. There was great rejoicing in our neighborhood. The neighbors said that children born near Christmas are a special blessing from God our Great Elder. On December 24th the twins were baptized. The local church custom was to baptize the twins immediately, since many died right after birth. Christians combined baptism with the African traditional custom of the naming ceremony. In this ethnic group, the birth of twins was a sign of bad fortune, but giving the babies names could protect them from the evil spirits. Since it was the night before Christmas, the two boys were given the Christian names of Emmanuel and John.

On December 25th the rejoicing and celebration at the twins' birth continued. Many people came to see the babies and congratulate the parents. Friends and neighbors brought gifts.

In my Christmas homily, I commented on the close parallel between the birth of Jesus and the birth of the twins. I stressed the meaning of the name Emmanuel—God is with us. I congratulated everyone on the double joy of this particular Christmas. First, the birth of Jesus Christ, our savior and redeemer, the Elder Brother who has "pitched his tent among us," and second, the birth of Emmanuel and John. In Africa, children are life and hope. Children are the future.

The celebrating continued on December 26th. Everyone was caught up in the happiness of this season of new life.

On December 27th the second-born twin, John, died late in the evening. How sad this was. Knowing how few twins survive the uncertainties of rural Africa, the local people expressed a certain resignation and patient endurance.

Early in the morning on December 28th we all went to Nchabukoroka's home to give him and Aurelia *pole*, the Swahili word for sympathy. I sat outside with the other men. Later in the morning, John was buried in the banana plantation behind his father's hut.

That afternoon I celebrated the Mass of the Resurrection for the dead infant John. We prayed for John's last safari back to the Father, the Creator and Source of all life. I pointed out that in our African tradition John was still a member of our community, now one of our "living dead."

That same evening Emmanuel died. We were numb.

On December 29th Emmanuel was buried in the morning. After the late afternoon Mass, I blessed the two graves with holy water. We walked away silent and downcast, trying to fathom the great mystery of life and death.

Death comes suddenly in Africa, especially to children. The twins probably died of pneumonia, since they were not sufficiently protected from the night cold. Many African mothers lay their babies near the warmth of a wood fire, but at night the fire goes down and the babies easily catch cold.

On December 30th we awoke to a bright, sunshine-filled day, but with heavy hearts. A deep, clinging sadness penetrated my being. Amid this paradox of life and death, I recalled the words of a Tanzanian priest who was asked what color vestments to wear at a funeral liturgy. He said, "My head says white, but my heart says purple."

True story, Father Joseph Healey, M.M.,
Nyabihanga, Tanzania,
A Fifth Gospel: The Experience of Black Christian Values
(Orbis Books, 1981)

A Slave Girl's Tears of Joy

Siwema was a young girl who lived in a small but beautiful village in the Livingstone Mountains near Lake Nyasa in Malawi. The sudden death of her father had left the family in crippling debt. Siwema and her mother were seized by slave traders in payment of the debt and led on a harrowing and painful trek to the Tanzanian coast. During the journey, the leader of the slave caravan murdered Siwema's mother before her very eyes. Siwema then embarked on a terrifying voyage across the Indian Ocean to the slave market on the island of Zanzibar.

There she was thrown onto a garbage heap by the slave trader who was disgusted by her ill-health. Just as a jackal was beginning to pick at her weak body, she was rescued by a young man from Réunion who took her to a small community of nuns. They nursed her back to health and she helped the sisters wherever she could. She received religious instruction, learning about God and God's son Jesus and his teachings to love everybody and to forgive, even enemies.

One night she had a dream in which she saw the cruel slave trader who had killed her mother and who had treated her so badly. He was lying on the ground, covered with blood. In her dream she went to him and killed him.

The next morning at religious instruction, Siwema learned the Lord's Prayer. When she heard "Forgive us our trespasses as we forgive our trespassers," her vehement response was "No, never! Never, never shall I forgive! For all the years of my life I shall never forgive him!"

Days later, Siwema was called to the hospital by the sisters. A British vessel had captured a ship of traders smuggling African slaves from the mainland to Zanzibar. Many of those captured had been injured in the fight. The sisters asked Siwema to clean the wounds of one man who was in very serious condition. When she entered the room where he lay on a mat bleeding, her heart almost stopped. She recognized the cruel leader of the slave-trading caravan. Hatred immediately welled up in her heart.

Then she looked up to catch her breath and saw the cross on the wall. She saw Jesus on the cross. "Jesus, did you die on the cross for this man too?" she wondered. Suddenly she heard herself praying, "Jesus, please, forgive me my hatred as I forgive him."

She was not aware that she was praying in a loud voice. One of the sisters was in the room. "Siwema," she said, "do you know that you were saying the Lord's Prayer? Do you know that you are *now* ready for baptism?"

Siwema cried, but they were tears of joy.

The next day Siwema was baptized and received the name Mary Magdalena.

Historical fiction story based on
material written by Father Paul Kollman, C.S.C.
and Father John Henschel, C.S.Sp.,
Bagamoyo, Tanzania

Could She Have Been Treated Any Better?

Josephine and David, a newly married couple who lived in Nairobi, were expecting their first child. They experienced a very difficult moment on December 24 when Josephine's delivery time approached. The neighbors were all busy—some preparing for the great Christmas feast and others campaigning for the coming general election.

They went to the nearest maternity hospital, where they found that there was nobody to attend Josephine, as the nurses and doctors were on strike and the watchman wanted a bribe before he would let them in. Since they did not have any extra money, they were sent away unattended.

On their way back home, they met a homeless family that lived on the streets. This family sympathized with the young expectant mother and arranged a comfortable place for her to lie down. Then they helped her with the delivery. Josephine gave birth to a healthy baby boy whom she and David named Samuel. Street children gave the newborn baby simple gifts, which even included glue, a substance much used by street children to escape the reality of their lives. Josephine and David were deeply grateful for the help offered by this homeless family.

If Josephine had been expecting the savior of the world, could she have been treated any better?

True story, Joyce Kaggwa, Nairobi, Kenya

The Faithfulness of Dr. Mayombi

There was a doctor at Bugando Hospital in Mwanza, Tanzania, named Mwana Mayombi, which means "the son of Mayombi." He encountered terrible problems in his life. First, his aunt who was suffering from cancer was brought to him at the hospital. While he was taking care of her, Dr. Mayombi received news that rustlers had stolen his cattle in his home village. So, he left his aunt in the care of the other doctors and went home to find out about the theft.

When he arrived home, he received a telephone call from the hospital saying that his aunt had died. "Bring her home," he said. The other doctors brought her body home.

While he was busy preparing for his aunt's burial, Dr. Mayombi got a telephone call informing him that a fire had gutted his house. His only question was: "Is everyone safe?"

They answered, "Yes."

Shortly after his aunt's funeral, he received a telephone call from Dar es Salaam saying that his daughter had died in a car accident. Dr. Mayombi told them to bring her body home for burial too.

After burying his daughter, Dr. Mayombi asked his father for a Bible. He opened to the Book of Job and read. When he finished reading, Dr. Mayombi said to his father and all his relatives: "When I came out of my mother's stomach all I had was given to me by God. Now God has taken back what belongs to God. My aunt died, my cattle were stolen, my house was gutted by fire, my daughter died. But I continue to thank God for all that he has given me. I'm not going to bother myself about the loss of my cattle. I will go back to work at the hospital."

But his father and his relatives tried to prevent him from going back to work before settling the case of the cattle. They said, "You should go to a diviner to find out the cause of your problems."

Dr. Mayombi's response was: "No. I accept everything as part of God's plan. God is in charge of my life, not the witches." Three times he said to his family: "Please let me go."

Finally, they agreed to let him go back to his work at Bugando Hospital. Dr. Mayombi was able to bear the pain of his losses through the grace of God. They called him "Little Job."

True story, Father Donald Sybertz, M.M.,
Mwanza, Tanzania,
"The Faithfulness of Dr. Mayombi," in
Towards An African Narrative Theology
(Orbis Books, 1996)

God Was Truly There with Us... Listening

One afternoon after returning from a funeral, Father Herb Gappa and I stopped at the Government Hospital in Bariadi, Tanzania, to visit a sick little girl that we had heard "was not doing well." She was about seven years old, and as we stood by her bed we could see that she was painfully struggling to take each breath. Something from the depths of my heart raged within me, DO SOMETHING! Yet, what could possibly be done?

Father Herb then turned to the family and me and asked if we could all pray together for this child. So we all prayed together. Again, for some reason my heart struggled within me to DO SOMETHING! I tried to formulate some small prayer in my newly learned Swahili as others prayed a few individual prayers. I unknowingly began repeating over and over to myself, "*Mungu, saidie yeye*" (in poor Swahili, "God help her"). I don't know exactly why I was afraid to pray out loud with my broken Swahili, but it was almost a fear that someone might hear my prayer and the struggle in my heart.

Father Herb closed our prayer with a blessing of the child and asked us to end with a song. So we sang. As we came to the last verse, this wonderful child of God literally took her last breath. I stood there in complete shock and sorrow. DO SOMETHING! Yet there was nothing to do but feel the pain and sorrow. After trying to console the family and discussing some sort of burial arrangements, we decided it was time to head home.

As we left the hospital, an old man walked out with us a short distance. He turned to Father Herb and said, "Isn't it amazing how God listens to our prayers?"

Yes, God was truly there with us. God was present listening.

True story, Marty Roers, MMAF, Bariadi, Tanzania

The Night before Christmas

It was the night before Christmas in Ghana and I was very sad because my family life had been severely disrupted. I felt none of the usual joy and anticipation of the Christmas season. I was only eight years old.

Christmas in my Ghanaian village had always been a joyous festival with beautiful Christmas music everywhere. Our church usually started preparing in November for the birth of the baby Jesus. Our houses were always decorated with beautiful paper ornaments made by the young people. The roads would be filled with people as relatives and friends visited each other. I remembered the taste of rice, chicken, goat, lamb, and many fruits. Oh, how I wished I had some of that food!

We always looked forward to the Christmas Eve service at our church. Afterwards there would be a joyous procession through the streets with everyone in a gala mood. Then, on Christmas Day, we would all return to church to read the scriptures and sing carols to remind us of the blessed birth of the baby Jesus. Later, the young people would receive special gifts of chocolate and cookies.

This Christmas Eve would be different. Last April the so-called Army of Liberation had attacked our village and taken all

the young boys and girls away. Families were separated and some people were murdered. We were forced to march and walk for many miles without food.

Miraculously, one rainy night we were able to get away from the soldiers. After several weeks in the forest, we made our way back to our burned-out village. Many members of our families were nowhere to be found. Most of us were sick and we were all exhausted. We had no idea what day it was.

The next day, my sick grandmother noticed a reddish and yellow flower we call "Fire on the Mountain" blooming in the middle of the marketplace. This tree had stood for generations and had bloomed each year at Christmastime. Somehow it had survived the fire. I remembered how the nectar from this beautiful flower had always attracted insects, making them drowsy enough to fall to the ground and become food for crows and lizards. What a miracle it was!

Grandmother reminded us that it was almost Christmas because the flower was blooming. As far back as she could remember, this occurred only at Christmastime. My spirits immediately lifted as I looked at the flower and then I became sad again. How could Christmas come without my parents and my village?

How could we celebrate the birth of the Prince of Peace, since we had not known any peace, only war and suffering? As I continued to think about the Christmases of the past and our present suffering, we heard the horn of a car. Several cars were approaching our village. At first we thought they were cars full of soldiers with machine guns, so we hid in the forest. To our surprise, we found they were ordinary travelers. They had taken a detour through our village because the bridge over the river had been destroyed.

They were shocked and horrified at the suffering and the devastation of our village. They said that it was Christmas Eve and that they were on their way to celebrate Christmas with family and friends. They shared the little food they had with us and helped build a fire in the center of the marketplace to keep us warm.

I noticed that my oldest sister had become ill and could not stand up. My sister was expecting a baby. But since we had escaped from the soldiers, she had been speechless and in a state of shock. I was so afraid for her, because we had no medical supplies and were far from a hospital.

People, including the travelers, removed their shirts and clothes to make a bed for her close to the fire. On that fateful night my sister gave birth to a beautiful baby boy. War or no war, Africans have to dance and so we celebrated until the rooster crowed. We sang Christmas songs, and gradually all the pain and agony of the past few months went away. When my sister was asked what she would name her baby, she spoke for the very first time since the village had been burned. She said, "His name is Gye Nyame, which means "Except God I fear none."

And so we celebrated Christmas that night. Christmas had come in the midst of our suffering with the birth of my nephew. This was our hope. Christmas always comes—despite all circumstances. Christmas is within us all.

Historical fiction story, the Rev. Peter E. Adotey Addo, Ghana

I've Spent a Long Time Looking for You

One morning when I went to say Mass at a mission chapel in Shinyanga, Tanzania, I discovered an inert baby lying in front of the altar. The mother, explaining that the little girl was dead, asked if I could say a Mass for her. Just then, the bundle moved. "She's still alive," I declared.

"But she's sick and I have no money for medicine. She'll be dead soon anyway," the mother replied. Giving the mother ten shillings, I sent her off to the hospital with the baby.

Seven years later a woman, waving frantically, stopped me on the road. Breathlessly she explained, "My little girl lived, and here's your ten shillings. I've spent a long time looking for you."

True story, Father Joseph Brannigan, M.M., Shinyanga, Tanzania

Maige's First Tricycle Ride

Maige Jumola is a fourteen-year-old crippled boy who lives in Mwanhuzi Parish in Shinyanga Diocese, Tanzania. His legs are shriveled to the size of short broomsticks. He propels himself using his hands and sliding along on his knees. I first met him three years ago. He never misses Mass on Sundays and special feastdays. He "crawls" the one mile from his poor hut to the church.

I always spend time with Maige, especially on Easter Sunday when his smile is brighter than usual. He joins the choir in having a soda after the celebration. He is not a Christian, but he enjoys reading about religion. I have given him some simple books in Swahili on the Catholic faith.

This year I decided to buy him a tricycle. It's quite unusual, with regular-size bike tires. The pedals are up front and are propelled by one's hands. When the parish priest and I arrived with the tricycle on the back of our pickup truck, everyone in the village turned out for the big event. Maige climbed on the tricycle and a big cheer came from the crowd. Tears of joy streamed down Maige's cheeks as he pedaled by himself. Spontaneous clapping followed him all along the road.

True story, Father Joseph Healey, M.M., Mwanhuzi, Tanzania

Yours Is the Kingdom of God

During one of the big celebrations at Mtoni Parish in Dar es Salaam, Tanzania, everyone gathered in the church for singing, dancing, and gift giving. In the front were chairs for the honored guests. In the very middle a special chair was placed between those of the outgoing pastor and the chairperson of the parish council. The special chair was for Cardinal Polycarp Pengo, who was expected to come for the celebration.

During the first dance of the Bakhita Girls' Group, eleven-year-old Simon, the son of the parish rectory cook, Lubango, came dancing up on his own, rhythmically swaying and waving.

Now, Simon is a very special person. From birth he has been mentally and physically disabled. His right hand is partially paralyzed, he walks with a limp, and so far he has not been able to go to school. He is a very good friend of Pastor John and also popular with all the parishioners. Simon is often around the rectory and he and John always have a good time together.

Reaching the row of special guests, Simon twirled around, "high-fived" Pastor John and jumped up on the cardinal's chair. The congregation clapped with joy. Even though the cardinal was not able to come for the celebration, there was Simon proudly sitting in his chair, smiling and waving through all the songs, poems, speeches, and the procession of gifts. It was as though the words of the Sunday's gospel had come true: "Blessed are you who are poor, for yours is the kingdom of God."

True story, Father Joseph Healey, M.M., Dar es Salaam, Tanzania

Joy and Celebration

*"If you can talk, you can sing.
If you can walk, you can dance."*
A Shona proverb from Zimbabwe

Joy is Africa's great gift to the world. Life in Africa means all-night drums, exuberant dancing and singing, wedding celebrations that last for days, and raucous celebrations of an exciting overtime victory of the local soccer team, national holidays, and big feasts like Christmas and Easter.

Most of all, life in Africa is the joy of people—a spontaneous welcome for an unexpected visitor, a beaming mother with her newborn child, the joyful response of small children when greeted by name, the ululation (a special trilling sound made in the back of the throat) of women and girls, a joyous beer party of the elders.

Despite the stark hardships that often accompany daily life, African people show remarkable resiliency and an ability to celebrate life. There is deep wisdom in the saying, "The poor celebrate best."

An African Canticle

AFRICA ....*BLESS THE LORD*
    And all you people and places,
    From Cairo to Cape Town all,
    From Dar es Salaam to Lagos all.
    Here let all the works of the Lord ....*BLESS THE LORD*
    Praise and extol Him forever and ever.

All you *BIG* things ....*BLESS THE LORD*
    Mount Kilimanjaro and the River Nile,
    The Rift Valley and the Serengeti Plain,
    Fat baobabs and shady mango trees,
    All eucalyptus and tamarind trees,
    You hippos and giraffes
        and elephants...................................*BLESS THE LORD*
    Praise and extol Him forever and ever.

All you *TINY* things ....*BLESS THE LORD*
    Busy black ants and hopping fleas,
    Wriggling tadpoles
        and mosquito larvae,
    Flying locusts and water drops,
    Pollen dust and tsetse flies,
    Millet seeds and dried *dagaa* ....*BLESS THE LORD*
    Praise and extol Him forever and ever.

All you *SHARP* things....................................*BLESS THE LORD*
    Sisal plant tips and tall lake reeds,
    Maasai spears
        and Turkana hunting arrows,
    A rhino's horn and crocodile teeth.........*BLESS THE LORD*
    Praise and extol Him forever and ever.

All you *SOFT* things ....*BLESS THE LORD*
    Sawdust and ashes and kapok wool,
    Sponges and porridge
        and golden ripe mangoes....................*BLESS THE LORD*
    Praise and extol Him forever and ever.

All you *SWEET* things...................................*BLESS THE LORD*
    Wild honey and papaws and coconut milk,
    Pineapples and sugar cane
        and sun-dried dates,
    Slow roasted yams and banana juice .....*BLESS THE LORD*
    Praise and extol Him forever and ever.

All you *BITTER* things ....*BLESS THE LORD*
    Quinine and blue soap,
    Sour milk and maize beer ....*BLESS THE LORD*
    Praise and extol Him forever and ever.

All you *SWIFT* things...................................*BLESS THE LORD*
    Wild goats and honking *matatus*,
    Frightened centipedes
        and lightning flashes.........................*BLESS THE LORD*
    Praise and extol Him forever and ever.

All you *SLOW* things....................................*BLESS THE LORD*
    Curious giraffes and old bony cows,
    Brown humped camels,
        grass munching sheep......................*BLESS THE LORD*
    Praise and extol Him forever and ever.

All you *LOUD* things.....................................*BLESS THE LORD*
    Monsoon rains on aluminum roofs,
    Midnight hyenas and feastday drums,

Train stations and busy bus stops...........*BLESS THE LORD*
Praise and extol Him forever and ever.

All you *QUIET* things....................*BLESS THE LORD*
Candle flames and just sown furrows,
Heaps of clouds and sunny libraries,
The Pyramids and Sahara Desert,
Land snails and crawling turtles,
Grazing zebras and stalking lions...........*BLESS THE LORD*
Praise and extol Him forever and ever.

All you creatures that never talk,
STILL BLESS YOU THE LORD.
PRAISE AND EXTOL HIM FOREVER AND EVER.

Prayer, Kilakala Girls School (formerly Marian College),
Morogoro, Tanzania, 1963

Why I Can Sing

Moro Naba, a Mossi emperor in Burkina Faso, had conquered a powerful ethnic group in the south called the Kasena. He extracted tribute from them once each year.

One year, at tribute collecting time, the emperor made the mistake of sending his son Nabiiga, a prince and his heir apparent. When the Kasena saw him with only a very small entourage of guardians, they overpowered the group and took the prince hostage.

His kingly robes were stripped from him and he was forced to walk around in only a loincloth. The prisoner received only one meal a day and was forced out into the fields each morning to hoe. Normally, manual labor would be beneath the dignity of a royal heir, so the Kasena made great sport of him. The women would pass by and belittle his manhood. While he was hoeing in the fields, the children would throw pebbles and stones at him.

But, to the surprise of all those watching from day to day, the Mossi prince would work and sing. He sang cheerfully with a loud voice as his back bent to the hoe from sunup to sundown. At first his soft hands blistered and then bled as he was unaccustomed to using a hoe. He lost much weight, but continued to be cheerful and to sing.

The elders of the Kasena were much troubled by his singing and buoyant attitude. "How can he possibly sing," they would ask, "since we make him sleep on the ground? We give him very little food and he is forced to work. Our women and children mock him, but he still sings!"

After a month of watching, they finally called him before a council. He stood in his loincloth, straight and proud in their midst. The elder spokesperson for the Kasena people asked the Mossi prince about his behavior, "Why do you sing?"

Nabiiga answered, "It is true. You have taken away my fine clothes. You have made me work, you give me very little food and you make me sleep on the ground in a common hut. You have tried to take away all my pride and all my earthly possessions. You have brought me great shame. Now you ask me why, in spite of all this, I can sing. I sing because you cannot take away my title and who I am. I am Moro Naba's first son and need not react to your shameful behavior!"

True story, Mossi ethnic group, Burkina Faso, Del Tarr,
Double Image: Biblical Insights From African Parables
(Paulist Press, 1994)

Smiling Rashidi Kikopa

Rashidi Kikopa caused me to break my solemn promise not to build any more houses for the poor.

If you ever get the feeling that life has treated you unfairly, just picture Rashidi, who lives in Mkuza outside of Dar es Salaam, Tanzania. He has elephantiasis, a form of leprosy, in both legs. Although he looks like a middle-aged man, he is only in his twenties. Both legs are grossly swollen and covered with large blisters that emit an awful odor.

Because Rashidi's brother-in-law kicked him out of their house, we are helping him to build a house of his own. Right now his new home of posts, lath plastered with cement and topped off with galvanized sheets, is two-thirds finished. He is already living in the house so that no one will steal the roofing sheets or doors.

There is no available medical treatment for Rashidi. Once he asked for an operation, but I had to tell him there was no hope. He smiled and left. Come to think of it, he's usually smiling when I see him.

True story, Father John Lange, M.M., Dar es Salaam, Tanzania

Celebrating Christmas in the Slums

Each year, people ask me how I will spend Christmas. I always answer, "In the slums." Sometimes I add, "You're always assured of one of the best liturgies in the world."

This past Christmas I was in Mukuru Kwa Njenga in Nairobi, the place I feel has the best Mass because of the powerful and joyful singing of about a thousand people. They make sure that the two hours they spend at Mass will be a happy diversion from their otherwise hard lives.

I arrived about forty minutes early and pulled the altar chair in front of the crèche to rest a while. I had said midnight Mass for the Little Sisters of St. Francis where I live and was very short on sleep. A big speaker inside the church was blaring Christmas hymns, but it didn't prevent me from dozing off.

I jolted awake. Where was I? Oh, of course, in front of the crèche. A little angel dressed in a pretty pink dress with a matching bonnet was leaning against my knees and fingering my hands. She seemed about eighteen months old, with big, curious eyes and brilliant white teeth. She saw a little sore on my chin and reached up to touch it. I whispered to her, "So you see my sore?"

She made an effort to climb on my lap, so I lifted her up. Her complexion was like smooth velvet. She immediately removed my glasses to get a closer look at my eyes. And then my ears. At times she just rested her head against my chest with the top of her head in the hollow of my neck. Then she'd explore my eyes and ears once again.

I spoke to Mary by the manger. "You have your baby and I have mine. What a precious Christmas gift you have given to me." I was in heaven for about fifteen minutes. As time for Mass drew close, I was wondering how I would get out of the chair. Just then, the cherub's older sister came and whisked her away.

True story, Father John Lange, M.M., Mukuru Kwa Njenga, Kenya,
"Christmas in Mukuru Kwa Njenga" (Maryknoll News, December 2002)

An African Prayer

May you, Lord, be for us a moon of joy and happiness.
Let the young become strong
and the grown man keep his strength.
Let the pregnant woman be delivered,
and the woman who has given birth
suckle her child.
Let the stranger reach the end of his journey,
and those who remain at home
live safely in their houses.
Let the flocks that travel to feed in the pastures return satisfied.
May you, Lord, be a moon of harvest and of calves.
May you be a moon of restoration and of good health.
Amen.

Prayer, Africa, used by CAFOD,
"The Living Spirit" (The Tablet, *3 October, 1998)*

Meeting the Holy Spirit in Stella's Smile

Many years ago, while still new to Tanzania, I met a very old woman of the Kuria ethnic group whose name was Stella. She was the nice old grandmotherly type. It was Sunday morning.

After half an hour of preparation, we were ready to begin our church service. As the opening song began, Stella came up and stood right in front of me.

I don't know what it was. I'm certain it wasn't the music, nor was it my Swahili or liturgical expertise. Nevertheless, I witnessed a minor miracle. Old Stella began to change right before my eyes! The wrinkles began to smooth out. Her skin softened and began to shine. Her cheeks rounded out to a beautiful smile that spread across her face. As the old Kuria do, she started moving up and down in rhythm with the music. Finally she let out the *vigelegele*, that traditional African trill of happiness.

Throughout the service, Stella smiled and looked so happy. Her mood was contagious and, little by little, we all began to feel pretty good about things.

As I sat with Stella in front of me that day, I could not help but feel a special presence in our midst. I began to realize the power and majesty of the Holy Spirit. As I returned to the rectory later in the day, I felt that I had been blessed. I had seen my God!

It's now eighteen years later. As I sit here thinking of evangelization, my thoughts center on Christ's Spirit alive and in our midst. My mind and heart instantly bring me back to that day when my old Kuria friend, Stella, evangelized me. For it was from that simple service in such a stark place that the Spirit descended. And, on that day so long ago, a young seminarian emerged with a fervent desire to go out and to preach the Good News to all people. How grateful I am to have met Stella and been blessed by her smile!

True story, Father Michael Snyder, M.M., Kiagata, Tanzania

Culture Matters

*"I pointed out to you the stars
and all you saw was the tip of my finger."*
Sukuma proverb from Tanzania

There is a vast richness, like the stars, in African culture, language, traditions, and customs. Africa's oral tradition of myths, legends, fables, and folktales plays a significant role in embedding and transmitting this heritage. In Africa, as in other parts of the world, the older generations, in particular, have been the primary transmitters of this culture. In the words of a proverb from the Ivory Coast, "The death of an elderly person is like a burning library."

The African experience can speak profoundly to critical questions about the meaning of life, suffering, peace, and human relationships for all the world's peoples. Stories from the past can respond to the contemporary concerns of people, and new African stories and sayings are also being created for today, especially for young people living in urban areas.

Perhaps some of these stories can help us see beyond the tip of our finger and as far as the stars.

How the Monkeys Saved the Fish

The rainy season that year had been the strongest ever and the river had overflowed its banks. There were floods everywhere and all the animals were running up into the hills. The floods came so fast that many drowned, except the lucky monkeys who used their proverbial agility to climb into the treetops. As they looked down on the surface of the water, they could see the fish swimming and gracefully jumping out of the water.

One of the monkeys noticed them and shouted to his companion, "Look down, my friend. Look at those poor creatures. They are going to drown. Do you see how they struggle in the water?"

"Yes," said the other monkey. "What a pity! Probably they were late in escaping to the hills because they seem to have no legs. How can we save them?"

"I think we must do something. Let's go close to the edge of the water where it is not so deep and we can help them to get out."

So the monkeys did just that. They started catching the fish, but not without difficulty. One by one they brought the fish out of the water and carefully put them on the dry land. After a short time, there was a pile of fish lying motionless on the grass.

One of the monkeys said, "Do you see? They were tired, but now they are resting. Had it not been for us, my friend, all these poor creatures without legs would have drowned."

The other monkey said, "They were trying to escape from us because they could not understand our good intentions. But when they wake up they will be very grateful, because we have brought them salvation."

Folktale, Tanzania, collected by Father Laurenti Magesa

The Lion's Share

One day the lion, the wolf, and the fox went out hunting together. They caught a wild ass, a gazelle, and a hare. The lion spoke to the wolf. "Mr. Wolf, you may divide the meat for us today."

The wolf said, "I think it best, sire, that you should have the ass and my friend the fox should take the hare; as for me, I shall be content to take only the gazelle."

On hearing this, the lion was furious. He raised his mighty paw and struck the wolf on the head. This cracked the wolf's skull, and so he died.

Whereupon the lion spoke to the fox, "Now you may try and divide our meal better."

The fox spoke solemnly, "The ass will be your dinner, sire, the gazelle will be your majesty's supper, and the hare will be your breakfast tomorrow morning."

Surprised, the lion asked him, "When did you learn so much wisdom?"

Said the fox, "When I heard the wolf's skull cracking."

Folktale, Nubian ethnic group, Sudan

Tell Us a Few Proverbs

An African king sent three messengers to ask a famous sage in a neighboring kingdom to tell them one hundred of his best proverbs. The sage asked the messengers to sit down and told them to close their eyes. For half an hour he said nothing. Then at last he said, "Tell me your dreams."

Puzzled, they replied, "How can we tell you our dreams if we have not been sleeping?"

He then sprang the trap by replying, "And how can I tell you proverbs if the situation has not arisen?"

Historical fiction story, Dr. Stan Nussbaum, Ghana

No Solos Please—We're Bantus, You Know

Some foreigners in East Africa are driven to distraction by the lack of competitive spirit among Africans. Tanzanians seem to have chosen cooperation and togetherness as a way of life. The first inkling I had of this was during a field day for students at a grammar school. Events did not include the shot-put, javelin throw, or even a tug-a-war. There were only foot races. After half a dozen heats of fifty-yard dashes, the Catholic sister in charge sensed that something was odd. She had a very hard time determining the winner of each race—the girls were all reaching the finish line at exactly the same time. Before the seventh heat, she asked, "What's going on here? Nobody is winning."

Oh, Sister," came the reply from the least shy of the youngsters, "it's better when we all come in together."

A similar story was told by a retired Dutch agricultural expert who had spent years in East Africa: "While I was training young men in dairy techniques, there was one clever fellow with bright eyes and quick hands. I liked the cut of his jib so much that, before I returned to Holland at the end of my first tour, I bought the lad a two-acre plot for raising hay. He was delighted at the opportunity to grow plenty of grass in the summer and then to harvest and store fodder for the dry season. Imagine my chagrin when I came back two years later to find that he had not continued putting his hard-earned skill to use. When I asked him why he had let go of a chance to get ahead, this bright young man replied, 'Oh, sir, you don't want to stand out and be noticed.'"

And I've never heard an amateur African musician sing a solo. Even when one person starts singing a melody, bystanders immediately chime in with harmony, counterpoint, and musical filigree worthy of Palestrini.

The cultural value of "not sticking your neck out" favors cooperation over star quality.

True stories, Father Lou Quinn, M.M., Sayu Sayu, Tanzania

Searching for a Symbol of Reconciliation

A Chagga man and woman got married in the Musoma Town parish church in Tanzania in 1991. All the arrangements for the wedding went along smoothly and peacefully. The marriage ceremony itself was a big success. Unfortunately, however, the organizers of the wedding had forgotten to arrange for a vehicle that would take the mother of the bride and her wedding party home after the celebration and feast in the hall. She was very upset and refused to attend the thanksgiving Mass and the family celebration the following day.

The leaders asked, "What should we do to make amends?" They spent two hours searching for a nice *isale* leaf to give the mother as a symbol of reconciliation. Then they paid her a visit. In greeting the bride's mother, one of the leaders handed her the *isale* leaf, a very important sign of peace and unity in the culture of the Chagga ethnic group.

Immediately upon seeing the leaf she smiled, expressed delight, called her relatives, and told everyone that she was no longer angry. She happily rejoined the wedding party. Everything went back to normal and the good spirits and close relationships continued as usual.

True story, Raphael Chuwa, Musoma, Tanzania

Father, You're the Poorest Man in the Village

Like all missioners in Tanzania, Father Jack felt uncomfortable about the gap between his standard of living and that of his neighbors. The local people were living in mud brick houses with thatched roofs, while he had a cement-block home with a tin roof. They toted their water from a well a fair distance away, while during the rainy season he collected rainwater in tanks on his roof.

One day while traveling, the missionary confessed to his catechist, Charles, how uncomfortable he felt living like a rich man among the poor.

In disbelief, Charles wrinkled his brow. Then he blurted out, "But, Father, you're the poorest man in the village. You have no grandchildren!"

True story, Father Lou Quinn, M.M., Shinyanga, Tanzania

An African Goodbye

Father Charlie Callahan, a pastor in Shinyanga, Tanzania, was dying of cancer. One Sunday night I received a telephone call from two Tanzanian friends, John and Monica, who were caring for him. The veteran missionary's condition had worsened and he was to be flown to Nairobi two days later. I called my friend Richard and we agreed to go and help with what was necessary for his departure.

On the morning Charlie was to leave, we waited for the plane at the small airstrip in Shinyanga. Charlie was lying on a stretcher in the waiting room, which was an open-sided shed located next to the landing strip.

I stepped outside and looked at the empty sky and the landing strip surrounded by high grass. Everything was silent. There was a feeling of great loneliness, of isolation.

As I walked along the landing strip, I could see that the grass was moving—even though there was no wind. Then I saw a figure emerge from the tall grass. It was a young child carrying a baby. She walked up to Charlie, who was lying in his stretcher on the ground, and made a small genuflection. No words passed between them.

I heard the grass rustle and I watched as more people emerged. Again, no words were spoken. Women passed before the stretcher and genuflected. The gesture ranged from a short dip to a full touch of the knee to the gravel-covered ground. Men passed and nodded. Soon the shed was surrounded by a crowd of people who had come to say goodbye. I was amazed by the silence.

Suddenly the spell was broken. The plane appeared in the sky and circled before touching down on the landing strip. We lifted Charlie's stretcher and carried him to the Flying Doctors' plane for his last trip. As I looked at him, he raised his hand.

There were no words, but his eyes were full of tears—as were mine. The plane taxied and was off.

For several minutes no one moved. The sound of the plane's engines diminished until silence again filled the air. Then, as the plane became simply a distant speck in the sky, the people faded into the grass and soon John, Monica, Richard, and I were the only ones left.

True story, Brother Kevin Dargan, M.M., Shinyanga, Tanzania

A Straw Fence the Height of a Person

In 1977, Michael Varga was a Peace Corps volunteer teaching in a village high school in a remote corner of southern Chad. After being bothered and hassled by the local people who were always asking for things—food, money, books—he had his students build a straw fence the height of a person around his living compound.

One day, a Chadian woman who was walking by started to scream and tried to kick down the straw fence. She had seen a dangerous snake crawl under the fence and wanted to warn the volunteer teacher.

When Michael heard her screaming, he came out and then together they killed the snake.

Michael invited the woman into his hut to have tea. Before leaving, she gave the him a charm made of animal skins to keep away the evil spirits. The woman then took the snake's body and cooked it in a special stew that she and Michael ate to seal the bond between them.

To this very day Michael feels that the Chadian woman's spirit is bound up with his own. He carries the charm she gave him as a reminder that it's very easy to close oneself off, to fence people out, to keep what you have just for yourself. Wherever Michael is, the Chadian charm helps him to fight that urge to build a fence.

True story, based on Michael Varga, Chad,
"A Straw Fence the Height of a Man"
(Notre Dame Magazine, *Summer, 1992*)

Learning from the Master

The Tanzanian villagers had invited me to a welcome celebration three days hence. As the honored guest, I would have the privilege of killing the cow for the feast. My brother, a missionary familiar with local customs, told the villagers I would be honored to do so. But I protested, "I can't kill a cow!"

During the next two nights of my three-week visit to Tanzania, I had bad dreams. In one I was holding a screaming, pecking chicken while trying to chop off its head with a rusty axe. In another I was chasing a big, spotted cow. In both dreams the villagers were laughing at me. Yes, I was truly scared. I had never killed a cow, a goat, or even a chicken. I was afraid that the village people would see me as a coward. If only I could start with a chicken.

The dreaded day came. While driving down the long, bumpy dirt road, I had only one thought in mind—"How do I get out of this?" As we approached the village, several people ran alongside the truck, cheering and yelling. I met the chief, who said many things to me, none of which I understood. The translator explained that the chief felt very privileged to have a brave and strong white person celebrate with him. The chief then asked me to choose the cow that most appealed to me. I picked a scrawny black one that looked almost dead anyway. As the cow was held down by five men, the chief offered me a rusty old twelve-inch knife.

At that moment, I had a flash of inspiration. Turning to the translator, I said, "I am honored, but I would much rather learn from the master." That made the chief's day—and mine!

True story, Paul Brown, Mugumu, Tanzania

We Africans Use Our Heads

I was showing a visitor around our local area in Tanzania. We hadn't gone more than fifteen miles when my Land Rover shuddered to a stop. I pulled out the owner's manual to try and locate the source of the difficulty.

We spent several hours at this, but made little progress. Then a truck pulled up and the driver—an elderly African—got out to help. He bent down and then wriggled under our vehicle while we continued to pore over the manual.

Emerging finally with a smile, he successfully started up the Land Rover. Meanwhile, a passenger of his was telling him about the splendid manual we had.

The elderly man replied, "The foreigners may use books, but we Africans use our heads."

True story, Father Edward Hayes, M.M., "Missioner Tales" (Maryknoll)

Did Jesus Christ Ever Kill a Lion?

A story is told about a missionary who went to a remote area in Tanzania to proclaim the Gospel among the Maasai, an ethnic group well known as a fierce warrior people. One day the missionary was telling a group of adults about the saving activity of Jesus Christ. He explained that Jesus is the Son of God, the savior and redeemer of all humankind.

When he finished, a Maasai elder slowly stood up and said to the missionary, "You have spoken well, but I want to learn more about this great person Jesus Christ. I have three questions about him. First, did he ever kill a lion? Second, how many cows did he have? Third, how many wives and children did he have?

True story, Tanzania, collected by Father Joseph Healey, M.M.

Seeds of God in African Soil

"God is a great eye
who sees everything in the world."
Arabic proverb from Egypt, Eritrea, and Sudan

This African proverb urges people to choose good, since God is always watching over them and good is what God cherishes. It reminds people of the abiding presence of God in all that they do.

God has been present in Africa from the very beginning of time, when the seeds of God were first planted in African soil. The holy ground for these seeds lies in the hearts of the African people and their cultures. Over centuries and generations, the roots have grown deeper and deeper, producing much flavorful, mature fruit.

God's seeds have produced such African values as community, hospitality, a sense of the continuity of life from the unborn through the "living dead," patient endurance in adversity, and solidarity. The stories that follow carry the bounty of these African seeds to the far corners of the world

This African Mary Understands My Swahili Prayers

It was the week before Christmas in Dar es Salaam. A Tanzanian mother was telling her young daughter Bahati the Christmas story. She took a Christmas card of a European painting of the birth of Jesus Christ from the table in their sitting room and said, "Bahati, here you see Mary, Joseph, and the newborn child Jesus. And there are the shepherds and the animals in the manger." Bahati nodded happily. Her mother went on, "If you pray to Mary, the mother of Jesus, she will always help you."

But suddenly Bahati frowned and said in a sad voice, "But I don't think this *mzungu* [Swahili for "foreigner"] Mary will understand my Swahili prayers."

Bahati's mother was taken aback. She went over to the table, picked up another Christmas card, and said, "Maybe you'll like this one better." It was a painting by a well-known Tanzanian artist that portrayed the scene of Jesus Christ's birth in an African setting. The cave or stable in Bethlehem had become an African hut with a thatched roof. Several sheep nuzzled the straw that the baby Jesus lay on. The African Mary sat quietly receiving gifts of corn meal, milk, oil to shine her baby, and firewood from her neighbors. Joseph sat attentively off to the side. A single chicken wandered around in the background. Bahati's mother sat waiting expectantly.

Suddenly Bahati's face glowed with a big smile and she cried out, "Oh, yes! I'm sure this African Mary understands my Swahili prayers."

True story, Perpetua Mashelle, Dar es Salaam, Tanzania

A Very Old but Very Good Joke about Missionaries

Archbishop Desmond Tutu of South Africa has a very old but very good joke about expatriate missionaries from Europe and North America. "When they first came," he says, "they had the Bible and we Africans had the land. They said, 'Close your eyes, and let us pray.' When we opened our eyes, they had the land and we had the Bible."

But the way he uses the joke, the tail has a sting. The Bible, Tutu points out, can be a very radical document and a powerful weapon, and the drama of his own part in the struggle against apartheid in South Africa is there to prove his point.

In the end, he maintains, Africa got the better end of the bargain.

True story, Edward Stourton, South Africa,
*"How To Be A Missionary" (*The Tablet, *5 July, 2003)*

The Person Who Couldn't Find God

Once upon a time a certain East African country had many mountains and valleys, rivers and plains, but all the people lived in one big valley. The large extended families included grandparents, aunts, uncles, cousins, and many children. These were ordinary human beings with both good and bad qualities. They followed all the seasons of human life.

A man named John Shayo lived in this large valley. He was a faithful Christian who prayed every Sunday and regularly participated in a small Christian community. He helped the poor and needy, especially the lepers who lived on one slope. From time to time he failed, but John tried to fulfill all his Christian responsibilities.

In this large valley there was jealousy, fighting, drunkenness, and all kinds of discord. Thieves and tricksters walked about openly and regularly stole cows, goats, and sheep. Witchcraft and superstition were part of daily life.

After patiently enduring this bad situation for a long time, John Shayo decided to move elsewhere. He said to himself, "God certainly isn't present here. God is the All Peaceful One who doesn't like fighting and discord. God wants peace and harmonious relationships in his human family."

Off in the distance there was a very high mountain that rose majestically into the sky. John Shayo looked at it and thought, "God our Great Ancestor must live in peace and quiet on the top of that mountain. I will go there to find God Who Dwells on High with the Spirits of the Great." And John set off on his long safari.

At the end of the first day he reached the foot of the high mountain. The burning sun had drained his energy. He slept and, very early the next morning, he started out again. After three hours of difficult climbing, he sat down by the side of the rough footpath.

After a few minutes John was startled to see a bearded man making his way *down* the mountain. They greeted each other, "*Jambo* ("hello" in Swahili). What is the news?"

John told the traveler that he was climbing to the top of the mountain to find God, our Creator and Source. The traveler said that his name was Emmanuel and that he was climbing *down* the mountain to live with the people in the large valley. After talking together awhile, they said goodbye in the traditional African farewell, "Goodbye until we meet again."

As John continued up the steep mountain, he thought, "That man is a fine person. He is very intelligent and speaks well. I wonder why he wants to go down to my former valley?"

As John Shayo continued his arduous climb, the air grew thinner and he climbed more slowly. By late afternoon he reached the top of the mountain and thought, "There is peace and quiet here. Now I will surely find God." John looked all around, but he could find no one. He was very disappointed and called out, "Where is God?"

Suddenly a gaunt old man appeared and greeted John. "Welcome. Relax after your long, hard safari."

John described the arduous trip and his desire to meet God the All Peaceful One. The old man said, "I'm sorry, but God isn't here. I live here alone. Surely you met God on the mountain path. He was going down to the big valley to help the people there with their problems and difficulties."

John was astonished. "You mean the traveler I met on the path was God? I didn't recognize him. I thought that I would find him here on the top of the mountain."

The old man said, "I'm sorry. You see, God doesn't want to live here all alone. He wants to join with the human beings he created. That's the meaning of his name: Emmanuel—God is with us."

John Shayo exclaimed, "But in the valley there is nothing but arguments and fighting. Many of the people are thieves, tricksters, troublemakers, and drunkards. Why does God want to live with them?"

Quietly the old man answered, "God knows the lives of his people and their problems and weaknesses. God has surrounded himself with simple, needy people just like the farmers and herders in the villages of your valley. He helps people with their daily problems. You can come to this mountaintop to rest and pray from time to time, but know, my friend, that God lives with the people in the valley."

John Shayo turned slowly. Seeing the large valley stretched out below him, John began to walk back down the mountain.

Parable, Father Joseph Healey, M.M.
with the Christians in Iramba Parish, Musoma, Tanzania,
"The Person Who Couldn't Find God," in
What Language Does God Speak:
African Stories about Christmas and Easter
(St. Paul Publications–Africa, 1989)

What Language Does God Speak?

Once upon a time there was a man called Marwa who lived in the Serengeti District of western Tanzania. In the sixth grade he studied the Christian religion. At his baptism he chose the name Emmanuel, which means "God is with us."

After finishing high school, Emmanuel read magazines and books about God. He believed that God was truly present among us, but he wanted to know what language God speaks. Emmanuel posed his special question to different church leaders in his village.

The old catechist answered, "I think that God speaks Latin."

The chairperson of the parish council guessed, "God speaks our local language Ngoreme."

But the searching youth Emmanuel had doubts. "When I get the right answer," he said to himself, "I'll know immediately and feel great joy." So the young African set off on a journey.

In the neighboring parish he asked again: "What language does God speak?" One Christian suggested Kuria, another local language.

Again Emmanuel had doubts. He began to travel across the whole of Tanzania, visiting small towns and big cities. In one place the Christians were certain that God spoke Swahili. People in western Tanzania said God speaks Sukuma, while residents in the northeast said God speaks Chagga. Emmanuel was not satisfied with these answers. Remembering the African saying that "traveling is learning," he journeyed outside Tanzania.

The Kenyans said Kikuyu and the people of Uganda said, "God speaks Ganda." In West Africa he got different replies: Lingala in the Democratic Republic of the Congo, Hausa in Nigeria, and Arabic in Morocco.

He decided to travel the whole world if necessary. Passing through Europe, he was told that God speaks French, or German, or Italian. The Christians of North America said English, while South Americans said it was Spanish or Portuguese. The young Tanzanian knew in his heart that these answers were inadequate. Determined to find the real truth, he went to China, where the local people insisted that God speaks Mandarin or Cantonese. Emmanuel was tired from his long travels, but he resolutely pushed on. In India he was told that God speaks Hindi. He reached Israel late in December. The local inhabitants said, "Surely God speaks Hebrew."

Exhausted by his long travels and the unsatisfactory answers, Emmanuel entered the town of Bethlehem. The local hotels were filled. He looked everywhere for a place to stay. Nothing was available. Finally, in the early morning hours, he came to a cave where cows and sheep were sheltered. He was surprised to see a young woman with her newborn baby.

This young mother said to the traveling youth, "Welcome, Emmanuel, you are very welcome." Astonished to hear his name, the young African listened in awe as the woman called Mary continued speaking to him. "For a very long time you have traveled around the world to find out what language God speaks. Your long journey is over. God speaks the language of love. God loved the world so much that he gave his only son so that everyone who believes in him may not perish but may have eternal life."

Overjoyed to hear these words of Mary, the young Tanzanian suddenly understood God's language of love for all people, for all races, for all nations. Emmanuel exclaimed, "Truly, today God is with us!"

Parable, Father Joseph Healey, M.M.
with the Christians in Iramba Parish, Musoma, Tanzania,
"The Person Who Couldn't Find God," in
What Language Does God Speak:
African Stories about Christmas and Easter
(St. Paul Publications–Africa, 1989)

The Muslim Prayer Connection

I went to the Egyptian Consulate in Nairobi, Kenya, to get a visa for Egypt. I had been told it would take at least two days. Another Maryknoll priest had had to wait four days. That same day I was starting a five-day retreat and then had a reservation to fly back immediately to Tanzania.

At the visa desk I explained to the Muslim immigration officer that I was starting a five-day prayer period that was as strict as the Muslim prayer periods, so I respectfully asked for a "same day" visa. He smiled and said that while visa arrangements usually took two days, he would ask permission so that I wouldn't have to interrupt my prayer time.

The officer returned to his desk almost immediately to tell me that my visa to Egypt would be ready in about an hour. And it so was.

It's nice to have a prayer connection!

True story, Father Peter Le Jacq, M.M., Nairobi, Kenya

Theresa's Old, Plastic, Armless Crucifix

One Tuesday afternoon I participated in the Bible reflections of the small community at the home of Theresa, one of the most faithful Christians in Bukiriro village in Tanzania. Following our local African custom, she had prepared a place for us to pray together outdoors. She arranged straw mats in a circle and placed fresh flowers in a vase in the middle.

Embarrassed, Theresa hesitated to place her only crucifix next to the flowers. It was old and made of plastic and had no arms. It had probably been brought to Tanzania by a missionary many years before and been passed around by several families.

I said to Theresa, "Don't worry. This crucifix is fine. I'm sure it has a special meaning for us."

One of the leaders read the Lenten gospel. This was followed by a period of silence and shared reflections. Suddenly it dawned on us what that old, battered, armless crucifix was saying. Jesus Christ was asking us to be his arms and to reach out to the poor, the needy, the sick, the suffering, the oppressed. Several Christians shared their thoughts on this, emphasizing the importance of mutual help in our local community. One person quoted a favorite Swahili saying: "Words without actions are useless."

After the Bible service, we helped Anna, one of our neighbors who had two sick children. We gathered firewood and fetched water for her while she stayed at home with her children. Like Jesus we tried to be men and women for others.

True story, Father Joseph Healey, M.M., Bukiriro, Tanzania

The Show-off Prepares for Jesus on Christmas Day

Once upon a time when Jesus was still in this world, there was an African woman named Kwiyolecha, which means "the show-off" or "a person who wants to make a big impression" in Sukuma, an important language in Tanzania. After hearing Jesus speak as no person has ever spoken, Kwiyolecha met him in Shinyanga town three days before Christmas and asked, "Lord, when will you come to visit us? I see you visiting other people, but you haven't come to our home yet."

Jesus replied, "Dear woman, just wait three days and I promise to pay you a visit on Christmas day."

When Kwiyolecha heard this, she was delighted. She immediately went home to prepare for the coming of Lord Jesus on Christmas day. The Tanzanian woman cleaned her house very carefully and decorated both inside and outside with many ornaments of the Christmas season. She hung colorful African cloths everywhere. She and her servants prepared special food and drink, especially the local beer. They slaughtered the bull that they had been fattening.

Having prepared everything to the best of her ability, Kwiyolecha dressed in her finest African dress. Then she sat down and waited for Jesus' arrival with joyful expectation.

Early on Christmas morning, a bent old man with sores on his legs appeared at Kwiyolecha's house. Upset at this intrusion, she told the man sharply, "What have you come here for? I'm waiting for an important visitor and I don't want you messing up my house. Go away right now." Without saying a word, the old man left.

Some time later, a very old lady appeared. She was dressed in rags and was supporting herself with a stick. Exasperated and angry, Kwiyolecha said to herself, "Why are all these things happening to me?" She rebuffed the old woman and told her, "Get out of here!" The old woman did as she was told.

Finally, at midday, a badly crippled Tanzanian boy appeared. He raised a cloud of dust as he dragged along his twisted legs. Kwiyolecha was very annoyed when she saw him and exclaimed, "What is this wretch doing here?" She said to the boy, "Get away from here and don't come back again." The boy immediately went away. Then, for the rest of Christmas day, Kwiyolecha waited patiently for the Lord Jesus, but he never came.

On the next day, December 26th, Kwiyolecha met Jesus in Shinyanga town and said, "Lord, why didn't you come to our home yesterday? I waited and waited for you. Why didn't you keep your promise?"

The Lord replied, "Kwiyolecha, I came to visit you three times, but you did not receive me. When you refused to welcome the bent old man, the old lady dressed in rags, and the badly crippled boy who came to your home, you refused to welcome me."

At first Kwiyolecha was dumbfounded. Then she remembered Jesus' words in the Gospel of St. Matthew, "Truly I tell you, just as you did it to one of the least of these who are members of my family, you did it to me." She began to realize for the very first time what it means to be a follower of Christ and the real meaning of Christian hospitality.

Legend, Sukuma ethnic group, Tanzania,
adaptation of a traditional universal legend, in
Towards an African Narrative Theology *(Orbis Books, 1996)*

I Had Lunch with God

A little East African boy in Dar es Salaam wanted to meet God. He knew that it was a long trip to where God lived, so he packed his bag with small, sweet cakes and a large bottle of soda and started on his journey.

He had been on his way for about ten minutes when he met an old woman. She was sitting in a park by the Indian Ocean just staring at some African birds. The boy sat down next to her and opened his bag. He was about to take a drink from his soda when he noticed that the old lady looked hungry, so he offered her a small cake. She gratefully accepted it and smiled at him. Her smile was so pretty that the boy wanted to see it again. So he offered her a drink from his soda. Again she smiled at him. The boy was delighted!

The little East African boy and the old woman sat there all afternoon eating and drinking and smiling, but they never said a word. As it grew dark, the boy realized how tired he was and got up to leave. But before he had gone more than a few steps he turned around, ran back to the old woman, and gave her a big hug. She gave him her biggest smile.

When the boy opened the door to his own home a short time later, his mother was surprised by the look of joy on his face.

She asked him, "What did you do today that makes you so happy?"

He replied, "I had lunch with God." But before his mother could respond, he added, "You know what? She's got the most beautiful smile I've ever seen!"

Meanwhile, the old woman, also radiant with joy, returned to her home in the Upanga section of town.

Her son was stunned by the look of peace on her face and he asked, "Mother, what did you do today that makes you so happy?"

She replied, "I ate small cakes and drank soda in the park with God." And then, before her son could respond, she added, "You know, he's much younger than I expected."

Parable, adapted by Father Joseph Healey, M.M.,
Dar es Salaam, Tanzania

It Was Time for Reconciliation

The words of Father Furaha rang out through the church in Kenya. "Go in the peace of Christ to love and serve the Lord and one another."

Alerted that the first Mass was now over, Maria stood outside the church door as the congregation streamed out. Mothers carrying babies, young people dressed in the latest fashions, and little girls in colorful dresses, protectively shielded by their fathers, passed by her. Looking down, she noticed two little boys pushing their way between the various tall legs to chase each other out into the church compound. An Asian family, regular buyers at her small fruit kiosk, stopped to greet her, while a woman with blond hair moved past, calling excitedly to her companion in some foreign language. Really, thought Maria, all races, ethnic groups, sizes, and ages must live here in Kenya. It is good to see many different people mixing happily together and looking so healthy and well dressed.

Recalling Father Furaha's words of the previous Sunday filled Maria with hope for her country in spite of all the insecurity, corruption, suffering, and poverty. He had said: "We are made in the image and likeness of God. Therefore, all life is sacred and each of us is of absolute value and worth. Jesus has not promised to remove suffering but has given us his Spirit and called us to help each other in our suffering." Yes, Maria thought, if we could only see each other as sacred and as a family, then our world would be full of hope. It seems that it is our inability to reverence and help each other as sisters and brothers that is causing most of our suffering today.

Looking at an old man who was the last to leave the church, she became aware of a new and deep concern for all life arising within her. Memories of last week's fight with her in-laws came back to her. She still felt bitter about the way she had been chased from their home, but it was time now for reconciliation and dialogue. It was time for trying to see all members of her family as worthy of respect.

It was time also for the country to throw away the sticks, the stones, the guns and spears and learn to live in harmony, caring for one another and working for justice in an active, non-violent way. It was time for reconciliation.

Filled with hope, Maria entered the church to offer all her thoughts to God in prayer.

Parable, Kenya, Kenya–A People in Pain—
1998 Lenten Campaign
(*Catholic Justice and Peace Publication, 1998*)

God Just Heard Us

No rain had come for months in Ng'wanangi, Tanzania. The situation was critical because the Sukuma people with whom I work here grow rice, beans, corn, and cotton—and everything depends on the rain.

Each day, I would join the women in our community in making a pilgrimage to the parish church, begging the Blessed Virgin Mary to intercede with Jesus to bring rain. And we weren't the only ones praying. One day we crossed paths with a witch doctor wrapped in a black shawl and carrying a black umbrella, a black rooster, and a smoking tin can. He was mumbling incantations for the same cause.

After a month of prayer, I had grown discouraged. Then suddenly it started to rain!

The delay was explained by a woman who told me, "Sister, heaven is very far away. God just heard us!"

True story, Sister Mary Dennis McCarthy, M.M.,
Shinyanga, Tanzania

God Must Love Us a Lot

Last fall we found ourselves in the midst of a spinal meningitis epidemic in the Musoma diocese of Tanzania, where I was working. Some of our people died within the first sixteen hours of exhibiting the early symptoms. Few of the infected persons recovered.

I visited Ngarawani village, which had been particularly hard hit. As I went from home to home, I tried to comfort the sick and their families. I had no great words of wisdom. I simply knew I needed to be with these people.

One of my visits was to an elderly woman, who, remarkably, was slowly recovering. We prayed together.

Afterward, she told me, "God must love us a lot. Fifteen people from our own village have been invited to live with God in heaven."

True story, Father Steven Brown, Ngarawani, Tanzania

God Is Like a Large Baobab Tree

One day my pickup truck broke down on the road from Maswa to Bariadi in western Tanzania. After I had waited for half an hour, a big Coca-Cola truck came by and the driver, named Musa, kindly towed my vehicle to the next town. This was a not-uncommon occurrence of friendship and mutual help on our poor dirt roads.

While we drove into town I sat in his big cab and we talked about, of all things, religion. Musa was a Muslim who belonged to the Nyamwezi ethnic group. In commenting on the tensions between Christians and Muslims in Tanzania, he said, "There is only one God. God is like a large baobab tree with different branches that represent the different religions of Islam, Christianity, African religion, and so forth. These branches are part of the same family of God—so we should work together."

Simply put, Musa gave me a wonderful African metaphor for world religions and interreligious dialogue.

True story, Father Joseph Healey, M.M., Bariadi, Tanzania

Glory Be to the Father

Glory be to the Father, the Creator and Source,
to the Nursing Mother,
to Jesus, the Healer and Eldest Brother
And to the Unsurpassed Great Spirit. Amen.

Prayer, East Africa

Holy Gospel According to Africa

After centuries of subjugation, famine, war, poverty, disease, and neglect, Africa still stands bloodied but unbowed. In time the world will pause enough to ask: "Africa, teach us how to pray."

Help us to recognize *Mungu yupo*—God is here—
as you do, in every moment of our daily lives:
    in the search for food,
    in the gathering of grain
    in the drawing of water
    in the sharing of a meal
    in welcoming a guest

in passing on to our children
the wisdom
    of our mothers
    and the ways
    of our fathers
    and the counsel
    of our ancestors.

O Africa!
    God somehow forgot to exile you from Eden.
    Maybe that's why, amid the sufferings of a thousand
        crosses and in valleys
    drowned in a flood of tears, you continue to smile
    and sing.
    And believe.

We missionaries thought
we came to you to share
our faith

not knowing that
all the while
you were making us
your own
and capturing our hearts
by your baptism
of desire.

You who walk the way of the cross
with every step and who know too well
the truth of our ultimate crucifixion,
announce to us today
the good news of salvation:
from the tomb of our good intentions
there arises new hope.

Poem-meditation, Father Joseph Veneroso, M.M., Africa,
"The Holy Gospel According to Africa" (Maryknoll, *March, 1999*)

Listing of Stories

To learn more about Africa:

Jesus of Africa
Voices of Contemporary African Christology
Diane B. Stinton
ISBN 0-57075-537-X

A comprehensive study of African understandings of
Christ that also includes the views of ordinary Africans.

*To learn about children at risk in Africa and
throughout the world:*

No Room at the Table
Earth's Most Vulnerable Children
Donald H. Dunson
ISBN 0-57075-491-8

The stories of children from Sudan and Congo to
New Orleans. Each chapter profiles three or four
individuals and probes an issue affecting the world's
children, including hunger and poverty, war and sexual
exploitation, homelessness and the need for love.

Please support your local bookstore, or call 1-800-258-5838.

For a free catalogue, please write us at

Orbis Books, Box 308

Maryknoll NY 10545-0308

or visit our website at www.orbisbooks.com

Thank you for reading *Once Upon A Time in Africa.*

We hope you enjoyed it.